KAYAK

D1119833

KAYAK

The Animated Manual of Intermediate and Advanced Whitewater Technique

by
William Nealy

Menasha Ridge Press

Copyright ©1986 by William J. Nealy

All rights reserved

Printed in the United States of America

Published by Menasha Ridge Press

Distributed by the Globe Pequot Press

Thirteenth Printing, 2004

Library of Congress Cataloging-in-Publication Data:
Nealy, William, 1953–2001
Kayak: The animated manual of intermediate
and advanced whitewater technique.
1. Whitewater canoeing.
2. Kayaks-Safety measures. Title.
gv788.N43   1986   797.1'22'0289   86-8526
ISBN 0-89732-050-6

Back cover photograph by H. Wallace

Cover design by Teresa Smith

Menasha Ridge Press
P.O. Box 43673
Birmingham, Alabama 35243
www.menasharidge.com

To Sheridan Anderson
1945(?) - 1984

You'll pay to know what
you think.

J. R. "Bob" Dobbs

Acknowledgements

Double special thanks for the support, inspiration and general crazyness, etc., to: Ocho Rios, Teresa Smith, Barbra Williams, Lynn Ikenberry, John Barbour, Steve Brown, Tom "Dr. Fun" Schlinkert, Gail Mesaros, Daniel Wallace, Tam Fletcher, J.R. "Bob" Dobbs, R.W "Bob" Sehlinger, Charlie Walbridge, Bunny Johns, Slim Ray, Ron Rathnow, Cameron O'Conner, Henry Unger, Carl Doggett, John & Kim at AeroServices, Emily Vickery, James Torrence, Paula Owens, David Smith, Reg Lake, Larry Hewitt, John Dolbear, James Jackson, Sue Stiener, the Women in Rubber and others far too numerous to mention. Extra special thanks to Les Bechdel of Canyons, Inc. for his help in translating Eastern Boatspeak to Western Boatspeak.... he's lonely out there in Idaho, so go see him. And finally, double extra special thanks to Holly Wallace who couldn't finagle the dedication this time but certainly deserves it anyway.

A mind is a terrible thing to waste
-unless you do it right...

Guide Saying

Table of Contents

NEALY BREAKS VOW OF SILENCE

ARCANE SECRETS OF KAYAKING REVEALED

API:Hillsborough, NC...Yesterday, in an exclusive interview, William "Not Bill" Nealy confessed that he had broken the centuries old vow of silence surrounding the little known cult of kayaking.

In an unexpected move, Nealy has offered the general public an illustrated guide to kayaking technique. When asked if this book tells you THE RIGHT WAY to kayak, Nealy replied: "Absolutely Not! It gives you lots of options but there is no one RIGHT WAY to do anything, especially kayak. This book is based on 12 years of whitewater experience. I'm no expert...I'm just an average boater who gets scared and swims and occasionally wrecks a boat. But hey, I always have fun and I can always say 'I did it my way.' Sometimes that turned out to be the wrong way. That's why I wrote it all down, so people can learn from my mistakes."

When this reporter stated that she had never before seen a book like Kayak, Nealy replied "**Absolutely Gosh Darn Right**! It's different. Why repeat a bunch of stuff on beginner level kayaking? It's been done. Kayak takes up where the others leave off."

Nealy goes on to state that even though his book is revolutionary, it alone won't make you an expert boater. "**Hey man, it's just a book, not a brain transplant.** My books aren't a substitute for personal experience. The river's a dangerous place and boaters are individually responsible for themselves. The main message of this book is safety and you don't have to read between the lines to get it."

As the interview neared its conclusion, Nealy began to pack his bags. I just had to ask about the Lear Jet in his back yard. "Oh, that. I need it for my research. It's the ultimate shuttle vehicle," he replied.

Flip Animation - Grasping the book in your right hand, flip thru book from back to front with your left thumb thusly...

The Low Brace Combat Roll ⌐

To boat or not to boat, that is the question:
Whether 'tis Nobler in the mind to suffer the
Cruel jests and loud derision from more
Courageous boaters, or to lay futile braces
Upon vast watery obstacles and by not
Rolling up, there drown. To die, to boat
No more, or by portaging to circumvent
The hydraulics and the myriad pointy rocks
That flesh is heir to; 'tis a consummation
Devoutly to be wish'd. To carry, not boat
For to boat, perchance to flip – ay, there's the rub...

Apologies to
William "Not-Bill" Shakespeare

Introduction

Some Dos & Don'ts of Modern Advanced Kayaking:

Do: Be Loose...

"Tight Kayaker"- fights the river... stiff... shakey... falls over on 6" riffles. Needs a beer or a valium.

Loose kayaker - works with the river... body relaxed... hull and body work with the surface contours of the river.

"Be Loose" is the single most difficult concept to teach a kayak student. If you're not loose, you *will* get creamed.

Don't: Shout and scream on the river unless someone is fixing to die or has been kidnapped by Bigfoot. Really... It's sooo obnoxious.

Do: give fisherpersons a wide berth. If they want to talk about whether they're "having any luck" they'll wave you over.

Introduction, cont'd..

Do : feel free to carry any rapid you don't think you can safely run. The object of the game is to have fun and not get hurt. If your buddies give you any grief, find somebody else to paddle with...

WIMP!

really!

Don't mess with the locals...

Cat

No, really... I think a river is the perfect place to dump garbage. I was just kidding...

Don't ever go "Wheeee!"

Whee!

Wheee!

This'll speak to them...

 # FEAR

Believe it or not, sometime or another all kayakers experience fear....unless they're very very stupid. Fear is a perfectly natural and normal response to what is perceived to be a physical threat to life and/or limb. Recognizing the whitewater environment to be ultimately hostile to human life, it's obvious we have to learn to control fear a good bit of the time. "Good" fear makes you think.. it gives you the courage to portage or the concentration to run a rapid you thought you couldn't. "Bad" fear causes panic, elevated pulse, irrational behavior (such as "going for it" when you _know_ you shouldn't, etc). A person experiencing a heavy dose of bad fear goes into preemptive shock (aka. "going to sleep", "zombied out" etc.), characterized by numbness, tunnel vision, inability to talk or paddle skillfully, etc. Preemptive shock is your brain's way of telling your body "Run this if you like but I'm gonna go hide in the basement!". If you think you're out of control and you maybe shouldn't try this drop, you're probably right. Learn to recognize immobilizing fear and channel it... it means it's time to carry.

Basic Precepts of Serious "River Fear"-

Zombie Factor One - "If you think you're going to die, you probably will."

Zombie Factor Two"- The time spent staring at a nasty hole is directly proportional to the time you'll spend getting trashed in it."

I _knew_ it!

Yiiieeee!

He's got 10 more minutes

poor Ed

Zombie Factor Three - "The amount of saliva available for expectoration is inversely proportional to the paddler's tendency to loose control." (ie- If you can't spit you should consider carrying that nasty rapid).

pffftttt

Introduction, cont'd...
Kayak Anatomy

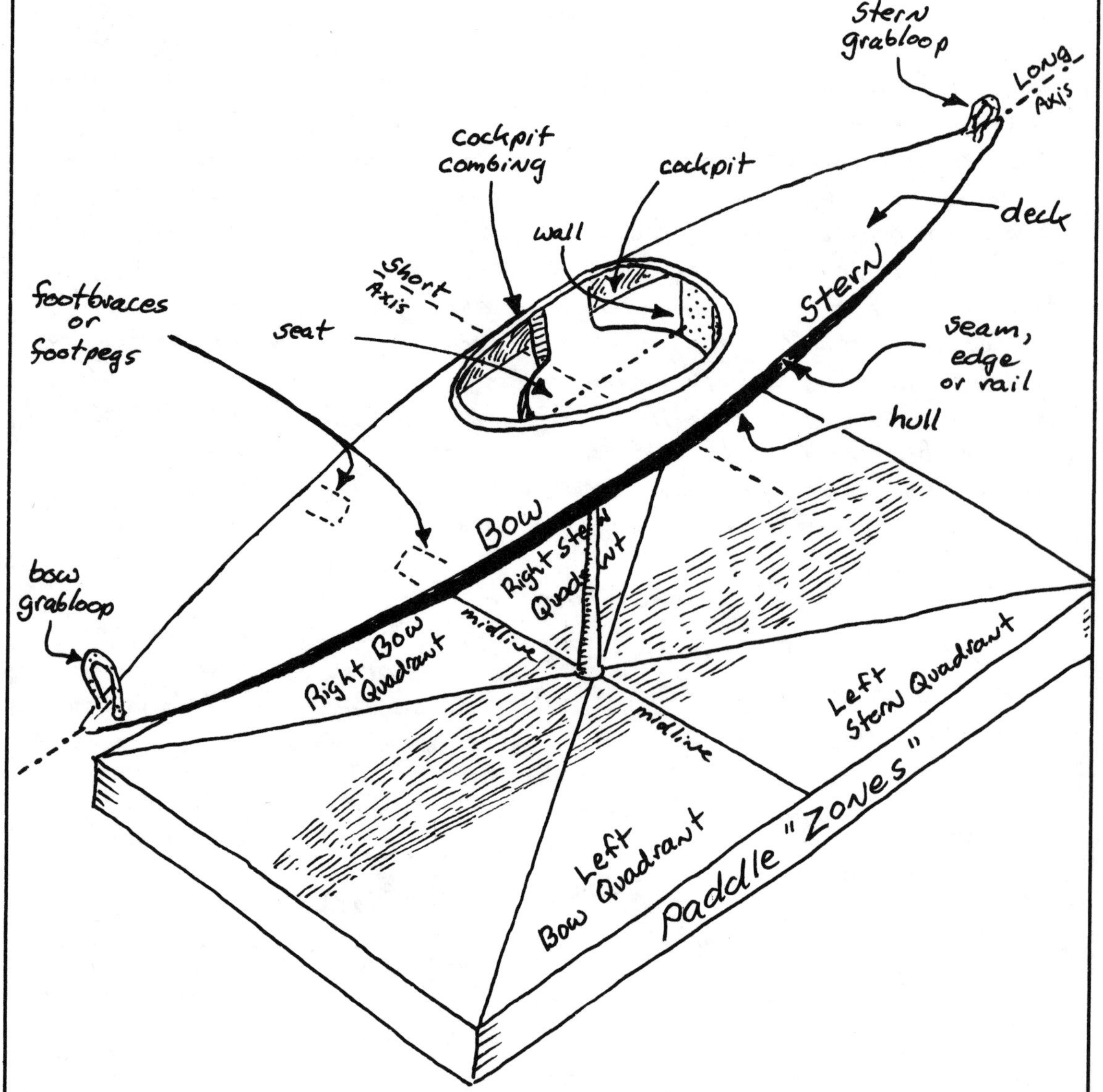

stern
grabloop

LONG
Axis

cockpit
combing

cockpit

deck

wall

Short
Axis

Stern

seat

seam,
edge
or rail

footbraces
or
footpegs

hull

Bow

bow
grabloop

Right Stern
Quadrant

Right Bow Quadrant

midline

Left
Stern Quadrant

midline

Left
Bow Quadrant

Paddle "Zones"

Rapid Anatomy

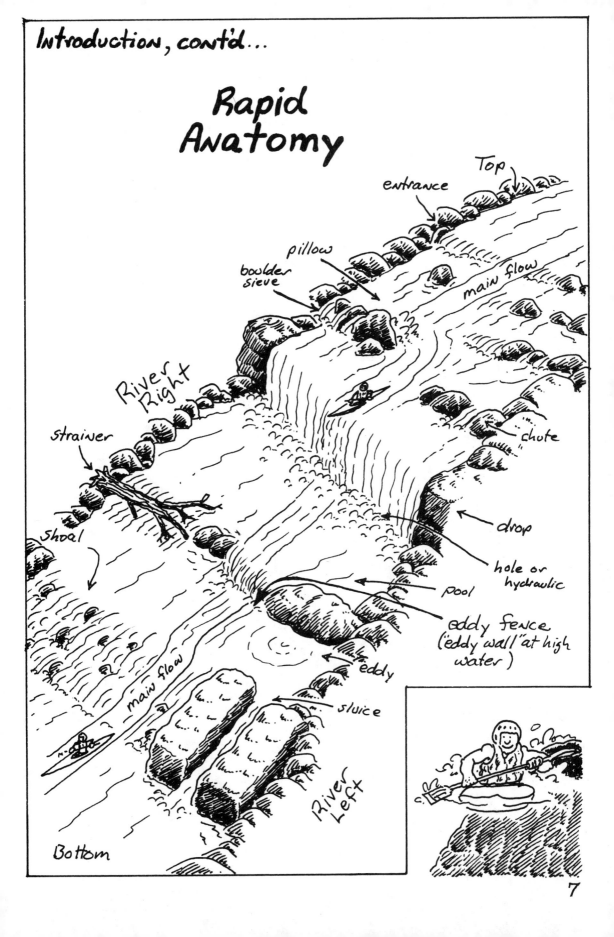

Top

entrance

pillow

boulder sieve

main flow

River Right

strainer

chute

shoal

drop

hole or hydraulic

pool

eddy fence ("eddy wall" at high water)

eddy

main flow

sluice

River Left

Bottom

Paddle Fu

(or "The Not-so-ancient
Art of Ninja Kayaking")

Paddle Fu, cont'd...

The true Ninja Paddler uses his/her whole body in concert with his/her chosen river vehicle to achieve perfect harmony with the river environment...

Anatomy of the Ninja Paddler:

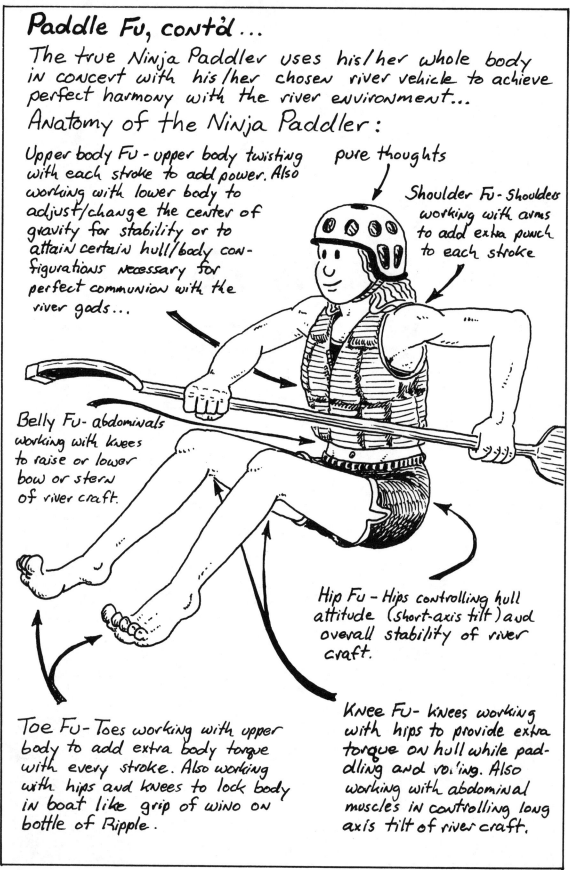

Upper body Fu - upper body twisting with each stroke to add power. Also working with lower body to adjust/change the center of gravity for stability or to attain certain hull/body configurations necessary for perfect communion with the river gods...

pure thoughts

Shoulder Fu - Shoulders working with arms to add extra punch to each stroke

Belly Fu - abdominals working with knees to raise or lower bow or stern of river craft.

Hip Fu - Hips controlling hull attitude (short-axis tilt) and overall stability of river craft.

Toe Fu - Toes working with upper body to add extra body torque with every stroke. Also working with hips and knees to lock body in boat like grip of wino on bottle of Ripple.

Knee Fu - knees working with hips to provide extra torque on hull while paddling and rolling. Also working with abdominal muscles in controlling long axis tilt of river craft.

Paddle Fu, cont'd...

Ninja Forward Sweep – Your hands grip the paddle approximately a shoulder-width apart. Beginning on the right, the right hand pulls the paddle shaft while the upper body twists to the right. The left arm straightens out in a shoulder-high punching motion that crosses the hull to the right. As the right blade comes out of the water the torso begins twisting back to the left. The paddle enters the water on the left, the left arm pulling, torso twisting to the left, right arm cross-punching to the left. Toes push on stroke side to add power (right stroke, right toes, etc). Paddle blade never comes higher than shoulders on recovery. *

Note egg-shaped paddle/hand path

Overhead view

*Ninja Reverse Sweep   same as above, only backwards.

11

Paddle Fu, cont'd...

Ninja Surfing Stroke - If you've caught a glassy wave you want to keep, the last thing you want to do is to add a lot of upper body fu to your stroke. In the ninja surfing stroke the upper torso stays still...only the arms move, in a circular path...

circular paddle/hand path

For faster, smoother stroking, slide hands in a few inches closer to the center of the paddle shaft than normal.

Ninja Low Duffeck - Beginning with a hard sweep, cross the eddy line and plant your paddle on the upstream side... lean over the paddle shaft and reverse sweep. If you've done it right you'll pivot 180° around the planted paddle and finish facing upstream.

Use Hip Fu to cock your hull toward the planted blade...the hull will carve into the eddy.

Follow through with a quick sweep on your opposite side for maximum effect.

Paddle Fu, cont'd...

Ninja Sweeping Low Brace - Starting with a low brace in the stern quadrant begin sweeping towards the bow while rotating the paddle shaft, changing the blade tilt from horizonal to vertical. Repeated in quick succession you get a kind of forward sculling effect... great for exiting nasty super-aeriated holes.

Reverse Sweeping Plant - This is a combination braking/turning stroke. The paddle is planted in the stern quadrant and swept forward by twisting your upper body away from the planted blade. The boat will stall and pivot 90° towards the plant side. Followed by a forward sweep on the opposite side, this is an effective (and dynamic) way to execute a turn in very fast water.

plant

sweep

upper body twist

Paddle Fu, cont'd...

Ninja Flurry Strokes - Useful for dynamic direction changes and speedy reaction to unseen obstacles. Flurry strokes are a quick combination of forward & reverse sweeps on opposite sides. To get an idea of the speed of a Ninja flurry, get in your boat and get going around 60 strokes per minute. Every 4th regular stroke throw in two or three extra strokes (bap! bap! bap!) between regular strokes without breaking your 60 s.p.m. rhythm. It takes practice but, ultimately, you'll get it down to a preconcious level. A "sweep" in a flurry is really a slap * - FAST! This is paddle fu at its best. Ninja flurry strokes are most effective in really fast water. They're also handy for staying on the crest of squirrilly waves.

*A slap stroke is just that... a slap. The paddle blade barely goes in the water. Slaps are mainly used on wave faces while surfing dynamically.

Paddle Fu, cont'd...

Rudder - Low Brace - Sweep - This is a stroke combination best used for surfing big tricky waves. The paddle blade stays in the water and is sculled into the various positions (rudder, low brace, forward & reverse sweep, etc.) while the paddler torques his/her body and boat against the paddle shaft, carving and planing* the hull on the face of the wave...

low brace

rudder

reverse sweep

forward sweep

*Carving and Planing the hull: A kayak hull interacts with water in two different ways.... When the hull is in full contact with the water it is planing, that is, skimming flat across the water's surface. Tilt the hull onto its side and it slices into the water and begins to carve.

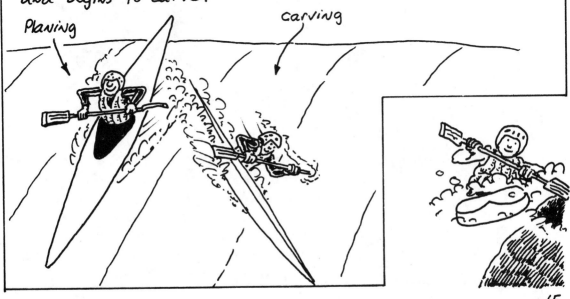

Planing

carving

Paddle Fu, cont'd...

Carving and planing the hull is done mainly by the lower body (abdominals, hips, and knees) usually in conjunction with upper body torque on the paddle shaft. While planing the hull on a wave or in a hole yields pretty much the same results (ie: stable position in relation to shore) carving on a wave is dramatically different from carving on a hole's "face." The moment you begin carving on a wave face, the rail is grabbed by the downstream flow and the boat is carried downstream.

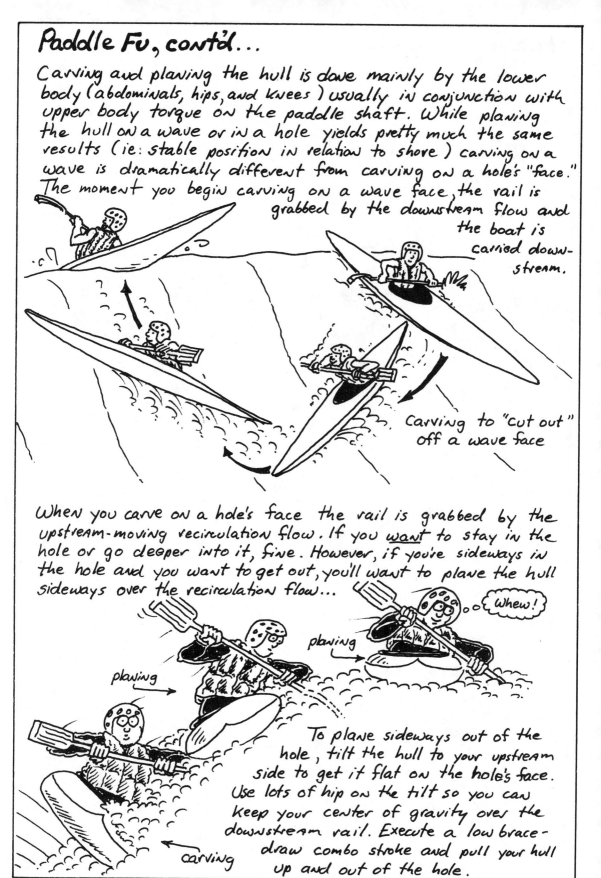

Carving to "cut out" off a wave face

When you carve on a hole's face the rail is grabbed by the upstream-moving recirculation flow. If you __want__ to stay in the hole or go deeper into it, fine. However, if you're sideways in the hole and you want to get out, you'll want to plane the hull sideways over the recirculation flow...

Whew!

planing

planing

carving

To plane sideways out of the hole, tilt the hull to your upstream side to get it flat on the hole's face. Use lots of hip on the tilt so you can keep your center of gravity over the downstream rail. Execute a low brace-draw combo stroke and pull your hull up and out of the hole.

Paddle Fu, cont'd...

Flying the Hull

Flying the hull ("getting air", "getting enders/endos") involves burying the hull underwater vertically and getting shot in an upwardly direction by water pressure acting against the bouyancy of the boat.

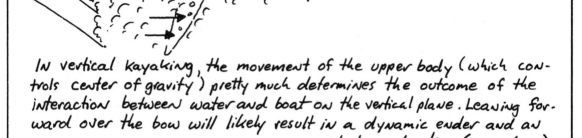

ya-hoo!

In vertical kayaking, the movement of the upper body (which controls center of gravity) pretty much determines the outcome of the interaction between water and boat on the vertical plane. Leaning forward over the bow will likely result in a dynamic ender and an upsidedown landing (see above)

Leaning back over the stern deck and literally standing on the footbraces will usually result in a quality ender and an upright landing.

Hydrotopography
(or " The art of using watery features to your maximum advantage")

Hydrotopography, cont'd...

For boaters, rapids are where the river changes from a two to a three dimensional environment. Entering a rapid, you're no longer skimming across a featureless plane... you are literally imbedded in a rugged undulating terrain. Waves are mountains, eddy lines are faults, holes are canyons. How well a boater can read the topography of this complex terrain and extrapolate what's going on underneath the surface can make the difference between a good run and a bad run, occasionally between life and death. Every new rapid you encounter is like a strange new machine... You've got to operate it but the instruction manual is lost. It could be a twinkie machine, a new-fangled toaster oven, or an atomic meatgrinder. Being able to look at a rapid and know what's happening both on and below the surface as well as how to react appropriately to the physical situation is the mark of the advanced kayaker.

Think of a river as a super-elastic conveyor belt passing over and under liquid rollers at high speed. The belt stretches and compresses carrying you along and (by friction) driving the rollers.

Hydrotopography, cont'd...

Of all the hydrotopographical features in the whitewater environment, holes make the biggest impression on kayakers. Some make a distinction between "hole" and "hydraulic" (hydraulic being a keeper hole). I use the terms hole and hydraulic interchangibly... the mechanism is the same whether it is a bona fide "keeper" or your favorite play hole. The difference is a matter of degree of severity. Anyhow, for the sake of discussion consider a hole/hydraulic to be any aeriated reversal flow on a horizonal plane [an eddy could be described as a non-aeriated reversal flow on a vertical plane]. Every hole is different and, like the lunatic yak jockeys who enjoy getting trashed in them, each hole has its own kinky personality. Below is the standard hole/hydraulic diagram applied to the conveyor belt model...

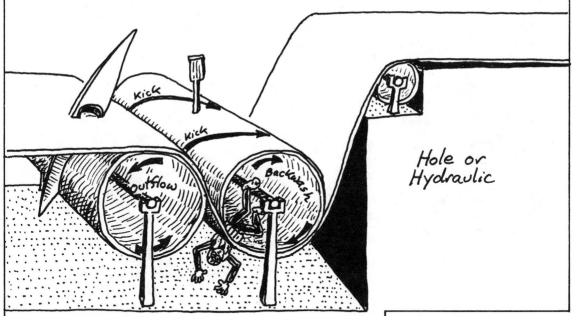

Kick

Kick

Outflow

Backwash

Hole or Hydraulic

"Kick" is the secondary lateral flow that all but the most symmetrical holes possess. A quantity of water passing over a perfectly even ledge into a deep pool will kick straight back upstream. Introduce any variation on this formula (angled drop in relation to the current direction, irregular ledge, irregular bottom, etc.) and the hole will begin to kick laterally to the downstream flow.

21

Hydrotopography, cont'd...

For example, a ledge angling across a river at 45° to the direction of the main current will almost always kick towards the furthest downstream end of the ledge (see below). A boater entering the hole from river left Ⓐ, will be kicked laterally to the right to eventually exit the hole at Ⓑ far river right...

If you can recognize "kick" you can predict what the hole is going to do to you once you're in it. Obviously the boater above would want to be ready for a strong left brace and an extended surf. Or run far right and skip the surf altogether.

The boater (Ⓐ) entering the hole below recognizes the left-to-right kick direction, throws a brace on his left and surfs out the right end of the hole. Boater Ⓑ wants to punch the hole and avoid being kicked right. She enters the hole at an angle that keeps her hull parallel to the kick flow direction... phew!

She paddles up & over the backwash without being kicked right because she kept her hull parallel to the kick flow direction... aha!

Hydrotopography, cont'd...

How to determine the kick of any given hole...

① Look for the main outflow (outwash). Usually a hole will kick toward where the most water exits the backwash.

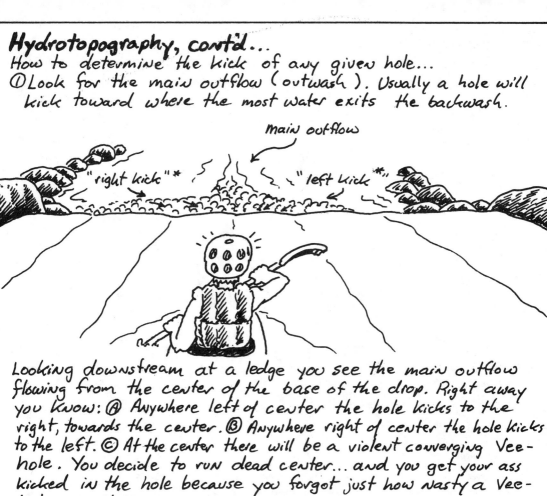

Looking downstream at a ledge you see the main outflow flowing from the center of the base of the drop. Right away you know: Ⓐ Anywhere left of center the hole kicks to the right, towards the center. Ⓑ Anywhere right of center the hole kicks to the left. Ⓒ At the center there will be a violent converging Vee-hole. You decide to run dead center... and you get your ass kicked in the hole because you forgot just how nasty a Vee-hole can be.

<u>All About Vee-Holes</u> - Where two opposing kick flows meet there will be an ugly-looking thing that looks like a giant toilet flushing. The opposing kick flows literally cave in on each other in a confused mass of seething aeriation. This is your basic Vee-hole. If you run dead center the opposing flows will crash down onto your deck, submerge your boat (and you), and flip you over in a New York minute.

*Note- "Left kick" kicks you left, "right kick" kicks you to the right.

23

Hydrotopography, cont'd....

The best way to deal with a Vee-hole is to avoid it entirely (unless you just _love_ getting trashed). However, if you find yourself looking down the barrel of one, set yourself up to hit just right or left of the maw. You want to hit the backwash parallel to the kick flow on a sweeping brace. If you angle the hull just right, you and your boat will climb over and out of the backwash, clear of the maw (see below, (A) & (B))

"Maw"

Right kick

Left kick

A   B

current direction

Now, back to our discussion on reading "Kick"....

② Look for structural indicators of kick (ie- is the ledge angled? Is there a "feeder eddy"*? Are there variations in water depth on the in-flow? Do the inflow and outflow line up?

Note- small arrows in backwash indicate kick direction

IN flow

OUT FLOW

Feeder Eddy

*A feeder eddy is an eddy below a drop that flows into the hole from downstream, adding kick. If there's a feeder eddy at bottom left of the drop chances are the hole will kick right.

Hydrotopography, cont'd...

③ The best way to determine a hole's kick is to trick a friend into going into it first. If your friend gets "displaced" laterally right, the hole kicks right and so on. If you <u>can't</u> trick a friend ("Go for it, Bob! I gotta bail my boat" or "Go for it Sue! I want to take some photos of your run.") a dry piece of driftwood will suffice.

This hole kicks right

Help!

Aiiieee!

Go for it!

Perhaps the nastiest manifestation of hole kick occurs below pourovers and upstream U-ledges.... In these instances the hole kicks into the maw from downstream <u>and</u> left <u>and</u> right simultaneously. In most cases this creates a genuine keeper hole.

Oh HECK!

Pourover

"Upstream U-Ledge?

Hydrotopography, cont'd...

Knowing hole kick direction is also helpful when performing hole extraction rescues...

A swimmer entering a right-kicking hole on the far left will recirculate along a spiral course towards the right. The rescuer can ferry along the backwash from left to right and try to help the swimmer as he/she bobs up at Ⓐ, Ⓑ, Ⓒ, and Ⓓ.

A boater stuck in a hole can use the hole's kick for a little bit of extra momentum to punch out of the hole by paddling in the direction of the kick. Conversely, a boater wanting to remain in a hole for a bit of surfing will have to paddle against the kick to keep from getting blown out of the hole.

Hydrotopography, cont'd...

Another useful hole attribute to be able to read is: "Is this monster hole going to keep me and beat the stuffing out of me?" The hydraulic nastiness factor is determined by several variables: ① If the hole kicks straight upstream and/or into the maw it's going to be bad. ② If the aeriation is "soft" vs. "hard" * you're going to have less hull bouyancy and paddle purchase. ③ If the formation causing the hole is wide and symmetrical (such as a riverwide ledge) it's probably dangerous within certain a.f.s. parameters. ④ If the ledge is slanting vs. vertical the hole will be, on average, grabbier than usual.

The only way to develop an eye for hole nastiness is to get in some holes and observe. Start with small, "safe" play holes and work your way up (down?). After a few good trashings you'll have developed some pretty good nastiness evaluation criteria of your own....

Hmm.... slanting ledge... kicks to the center.... aeriation soft to medium.... three boatlengths wide....ledge smooth and symmetrical...

help!

*See p. 40
"Reading Aeriation"

On big water or floodstage rivers all bets are off... hole nastiness evaluation becomes a form of voodoo. In general, the less aeriated the hole the better your chances of survival. One semi-comforting thing to remember is that if you bail out you'll probably flush under the backwash and come up a ways downstream. Unless you've aspirated half the river or been bounced across the bottom, you'll be none the worse for wear If rescue is quick. Exceptions to big water flush-through are: low head dams, double undercut ledges, wide slanting ledges, deeply undercut ledges, the like. Remember: one man's (or woman's) playhole can be another man's (or woman's) worst nightmare....

Hydrotopography, cont'd... Reef-er Madness

A reef is a big river-wide slanting drop covered with an inch or two of water. Geologically speaking, reefs are intrusions of hard rock left behind when softer surrounding rock eroded away. A reef causes a natural damming effect with a deep pool on the upstream side and a relatively shallow pool on the downstream side. Unlike the smoother water-sculpted surrounding rock, the reef is apt to have a rough, jagged surface...

Reef Evolution

On the river the most important consideration is this: a reef is basically a big damp rock with a rough surface and sharp protrusions that may rip up or hang up you _and_ your boat. When scouting a reef, think to yourself "If this was a big slanting rock hanging over a pool, would I slide off the sucker?" If "yes", then you've got to "read" the reef and answer the following questions in order to find a safe line down: Ⓐ Are there sharp jagged protrusions pointed upstream that will cause me to hang up, or worse cause me and my boat to be literally shredded into tiny bits before I bottom out? Ⓑ If I make it to the bottom, is the water deep and unobstructed so's I don't get vertically pinned?

To answer Ⓐ, "Is this reef a natural cheese-grater?", look at the face... upstream protrusions and sharp edges will create distinct highly-aeriated mini-holes and little roostertails. If the whole face is aeriated and violent, carry it!

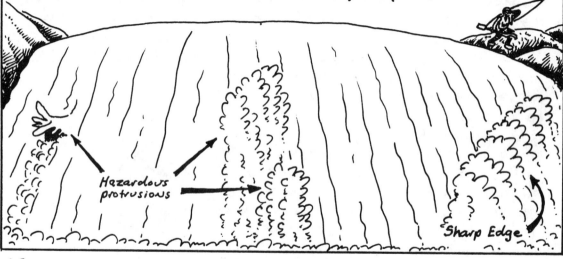

Hazardous protrusions

Sharp Edge

Hydrotopography, cont'd...

Your line should be clear of edges and protusions, as well as being nearly perfectly vertical. When (if) you find a good line it's time to closely examine your landing spot and answer question Ⓑ (preceding page).

Pinning Rock

"Safe" Line

Uniform, non-violent aeriated hole indicates relatively deep water with no submerged obstructions

Shallow water.. Submerged Rocks!!

Once you've picked a satisfactory line, the next (final) scouting step is to pick out downstream markers from upstream so you can triangulate from the cockpit and line up accurately.

..from the eddy aim for the tree and hit the horizon line one boatlength off the right shore...

Hydrotopography, cont'd..

Run a reef just like sliding off a big rock (ie: forget the reef current). Keep the bow pointed straight down the fall line. Hold your paddle in low brace position to use as a stabilizer if you start to flip. Unless you know for an Absolute Fact that your landing spot is plenty deep and free from obstructions, go slow when nearing the lip... backpaddle if necessary. The slower you bottom out the less likely you'll pencil into the bottom and/or pin on any submerged rocks lurking under the aeriation. Control, not speed*, is the essence of safe reef-running.

[*Since most reef-caused holes are relatively weak, speed is unnecessary.]

When you bottom out lean way back and back brace on either side to quickly raise the bow clear of bottom obstructions.

NEVER drag your paddle on edge on a reef (or anywhere else for that matter). Your tip may chock in a crack resulting in a broken paddle, wrenched shoulders, sprained wrists and a spectacular crash and burn...

what th' fu..

Hydrotopography, cont'd...

Folded Flows - A folded flow usually occurs where a river flows over an upstream-angled V-shaped ledge. Where the two walls of falling water meet, one actually flows over the other creating a "fold". The Chattooga's Seven Foot Falls is a classic example of a folded flow.

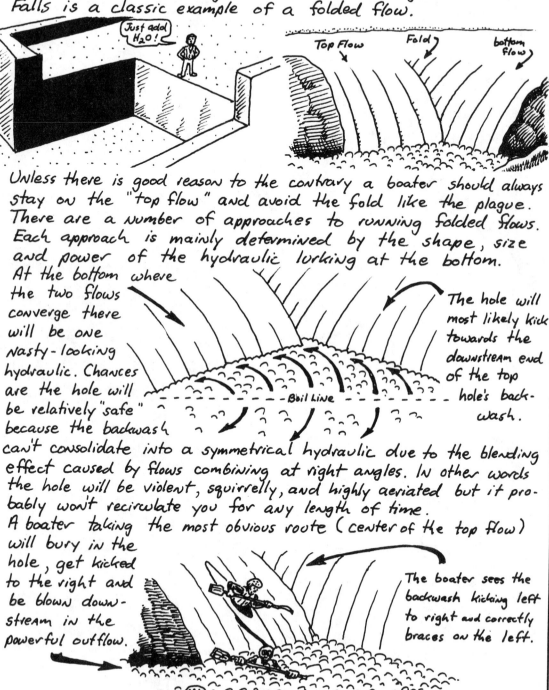

Just add H₂O!

Top Flow   Fold   bottom flow

Unless there is good reason to the contrary a boater should always stay on the "top flow" and avoid the fold like the plague. There are a number of approaches to running folded flows. Each approach is mainly determined by the shape, size and power of the hydraulic lurking at the bottom.

At the bottom where the two flows converge there will be one nasty-looking hydraulic. Chances are the hole will be relatively "safe" because the backwash can't consolidate into a symmetrical hydraulic due to the blending effect caused by flows combining at right angles. In other words the hole will be violent, squirrelly, and highly aeriated but it probably won't recirculate you for any length of time.

The hole will most likely kick towards the downstream end of the top hole's back-wash.

- - - Boil Line - - -

A boater taking the most obvious route (center of the top flow) will bury in the hole, get kicked to the right and be blown downstream in the powerful outflow.

The boater sees the backwash kicking left to right and correctly braces on the left.

32

Hydrotopography, cont'd...

The hole can be avoided completely by running diagonally across the top flow at high speed...

If for some reason you're unable (or unwilling) to run the top flow, consider the bottom flow. As long as you stay clear of the fold (and the hole isn't terminal) running center on the bottom flow is a good alternative. You will probably get kicked to the right and into the top flow's backwash and, eventually, out.

If you screw up and blunder into the fold, here's what's going to happen...

Hydrotopography, cont'd...
Waterfalls, Big Drops

There are about as many types of waterfalls* as there are waterfalls. Each one is different and, like the weirdos who run them, each has its own bizzare personality. Everybody has his/her own pre-run waterfall ritual.... some automatically carry the drop... some go into a state of ecstasy... some (myself included) become zombies... some pray to the appropriate diety (dieties).

To keep the zombie trance at bay I analyze the physical situation and try to answer the following questions: ① Is there a clean descent line? ② Can I hit my chosen line? (Is the approach straight-forward?) ③ Will I arrive at the bottom up-right and intact? ④ Is the bottom hole deep & unobstructed so's I don't get pinned or crunch my bow? ⑤ Once in the hole will I be home for Christmas? (In other words, will the hole let me go?) ⑥ If I get trashed, can somebody rescue me? ⑦ What's directly downstream... could I swim it and sustain only minor injuries? And finally.. ⑧ Am I physically & mentally capable of running this mother? [Zombie Factor #1*]. If I can answer "definitely yes" (or at least "definitely maybe") to each and every question, I'll run the drop, (unless it starts to rain or I start throwing up). If there's one "NO" or too many "maybes" I'll be portaging. Like all kayakers, I have a natural aversion to both carrying anything <u>and</u> looking like a wimp to my fellow boaters. But, after much serious thought on the matter, I've concluded that it is far better to be a healthy wimp than a dead or damaged hero. Running big drops is big fun but I'll pass on the puberty rites, thanks....

* For the sake of discussion, any vertical drop of 8' or more is referred to here as "waterfall" or "drop" interchangeably.

* Zombie Factor One - "If you think you're going to die, you probably will." [See "Fear" pp 5]

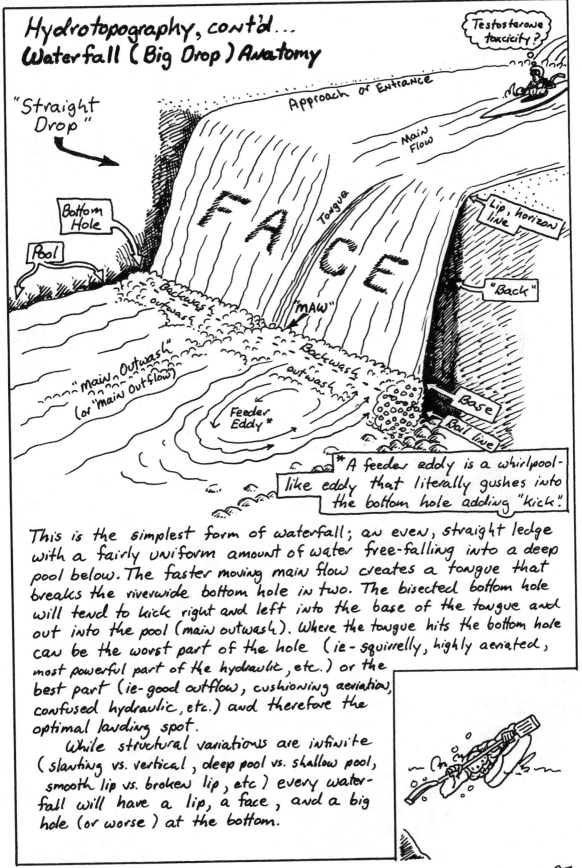

Hydrotopography, cont'd...
Waterfall (Big Drop) Anatomy

Testosterone toxcicity?

Approach or Entrance

Main Flow

"Straight Drop"

Tongue

F A C E

Lip, horizon line

Bottom Hole

Pool

"Back"

Outwash

"MAW"

Backwash outwash

Base

"main Outwash" (or "main Outflow")

Feeder Eddy *

Boil line

*A feeder eddy is a whirlpool-like eddy that literally gushes into the bottom hole adding "kick"!

This is the simplest form of waterfall; an even, straight ledge with a fairly uniform amount of water free-falling into a deep pool below. The faster moving main flow creates a tongue that breaks the riverwide bottom hole in two. The bisected bottom hole will tend to kick right and left into the base of the tongue and out into the pool (main outwash). Where the tongue hits the bottom hole can be the worst part of the hole (ie-squirrelly, highly aeriated, most powerful part of the hydraulic, etc.) or the best part (ie-good outflow, cushioning aeriation, confused hydraulic, etc.) and therefore the optimal landing spot.

While structural variations are infinite (slanting vs. vertical, deep pool vs. shallow pool, smooth lip vs. broken lip, etc) every water-fall will have a lip, a face, and a big hole (or worse) at the bottom.

Hydrotopography, cont'd...
Basic Waterfall Typology:

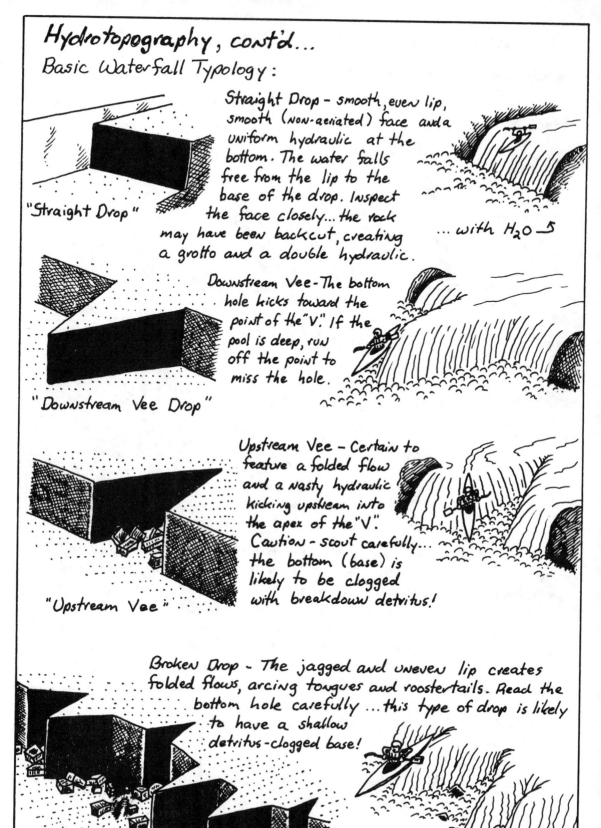

Straight Drop - smooth, even lip, smooth (non-aeriated) face and a uniform hydraulic at the bottom. The water falls free from the lip to the base of the drop. Inspect the face closely... the rock may have been backcut, creating a grotto and a double hydraulic.

"Straight Drop"

... with H_2O ⌐

Downstream Vee - The bottom hole kicks toward the point of the "V." If the pool is deep, run off the point to miss the hole.

"Downstream Vee Drop"

Upstream Vee - Certain to feature a folded flow and a nasty hydraulic kicking upstream into the apex of the "V." Caution - scout carefully... the bottom (base) is likely to be clogged with breakdown detritus!

"Upstream Vee"

Broken Drop - The jagged and uneven lip creates folded flows, arcing tongues and roostertails. Read the bottom hole carefully ... this type of drop is likely to have a shallow detritus-clogged base!

"Broken Drop".

36

Hydrotopography, cont'd...
Basic Waterfall Typology...

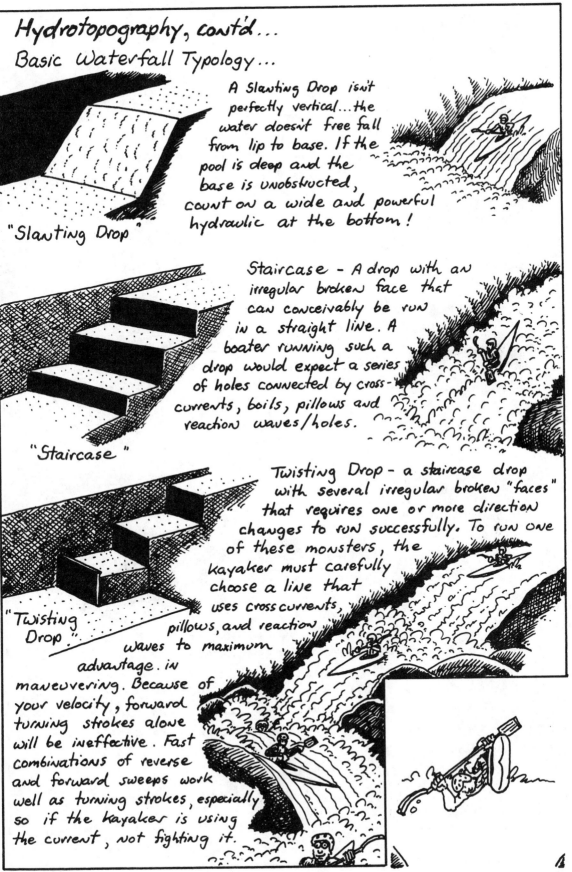

A Slanting Drop isn't perfectly vertical...the water doesn't free fall from lip to base. If the pool is deep and the base is unobstructed, count on a wide and powerful hydraulic at the bottom!

"Slanting Drop"

Staircase - A drop with an irregular broken face that can conceivably be run in a straight line. A boater running such a drop would expect a series of holes connected by cross-currents, boils, pillows and reaction waves/holes.

"Staircase"

Twisting Drop - a staircase drop with several irregular broken "faces" that requires one or more direction changes to run successfully. To run one of these monsters, the kayaker must carefully choose a line that uses cross currents, pillows, and reaction waves to maximum advantage. in maneuvering. Because of your velocity, forward turning strokes alone will be ineffective. Fast combinations of reverse and forward sweeps work well as turning strokes, especially so if the kayaker is using the current, not fighting it.

"Twisting Drop"

Hydrotopography, cont'd...

...more typology

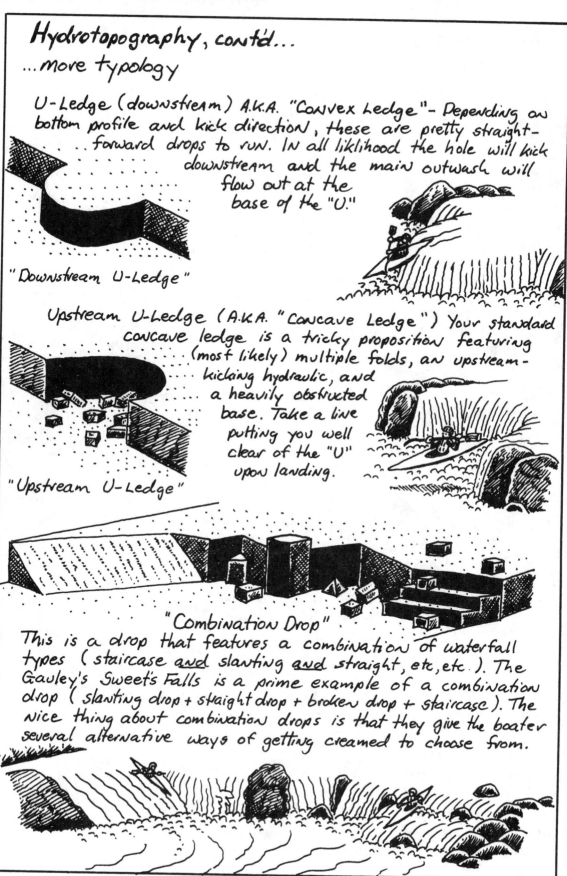

U-Ledge (downstream) A.K.A. "Convex Ledge"- Depending on bottom profile and kick direction, these are pretty straight-forward drops to run. In all liklihood the hole will kick downstream and the main outwash will flow out at the base of the "U."

"Downstream U-Ledge"

Upstream U-Ledge (A.K.A. "Concave Ledge") Your standard concave ledge is a tricky proposition featuring (most likely) multiple folds, an upstream-kicking hydraulic, and a heavily obstructed base. Take a line putting you well clear of the "U" upon landing.

"Upstream U-Ledge"

"Combination Drop"

This is a drop that features a combination of waterfall types (staircase and slanting and straight, etc, etc.). The Gauley's Sweet's Falls is a prime example of a combination drop (slanting drop + straight drop + broken drop + staircase). The nice thing about combination drops is that they give the boater several alternative ways of getting creamed to choose from.

Hydrotopography, cont'd...
...plus some extra information...

Backcut Ledge — Sometimes the rock forming a waterfall is composed of a layer of "hard" cap rock overlying layers of softer rock. The forces generated by the falling water hitting the pool begin to erode the face of the drop creating an upstream undercut ("grotto"). Given extensive backcutting, a double hydraulic will form presenting a significant hazard to boaters. To make matters worse, driftwood & debris can end up jammed into the backcut creating a hydraulic/strainer. When possible, check behind the face of waterfalls for signs of backcutting. In addition, when a backcut ledge features a strong tongue (or "plume") there will be a bizzare doughnut-shaped hydraulic where the tongue strikes the pool.

Backcut or grotto

Hard Rock

Soft Rock

Double Hydraulic

Enough typology already! What does all this mean to me?

I want to know how to actually run one of these suckers!

Soon, dear reader. Soon...

Hydrotopography, cont'd...
but first.... Reading Aeriation

Reading aeriation is, at best, a very inexact science. I've been doing it for over a decade and I'm only right about half the time. The purpose of reading aeriation is to find out what's going to happen to you at the bottom of the drop. Aeriation is the result of air being forcefully mixed with water where opposing flows meet. Correct interpretation of aeriation will tell you approximate water depth, hole strength & shape, whether or not invisible obstructions are present, where you'll be going when you land, whether or not you'll bury in the hole, and whether or not you'll be able to surf and brace in the hole if you get caught. The Nealy scale of relative aeriation hardness goes from Soft (fizzy-foamy) to Hard (splashy-percolating). Soft aeriation has a high air-to-water mix ratio, (whereas hard aeriation has a low air/water mix ratio). Soft aeriation is made up of tiny air bubbles and is pure white. It looks like soap suds and kind of flops upstream into the interface. The boil and outwash will look like a high-budget Alka Seltzer commercial ("fizz" "pop!"). The good news is... soft aeriation means fairly deep water, a smooth unobstructed bottom, and a well-cushioned landing spot. The bad news is soft aeriation also means a very squirrelly hard-to-surf backwash, and a well-formed uniform (and thus _powerful_!) hydraulic. A kayaker landing in soft aeriation will bury deep into the froth and bob up in water that won't "take" a brace. The only way to brace in soft aeriation is to scull like crazy while keeping your hull under you. Regular side-surfing (hull on edge, torso downstream) will result in an instant flip. The high air to water mix literally makes your hull less bouyant. Turn the hull on edge and it will sink like a red-hot anvil in a vat of Velveeta. A swimmer in this stuff may surface (if at all) only every other recycle.

Hydrotopography, cont'd...

If a hazard is hidden under soft aeriation it will "show" by causing boils, humps, & irregularities in the backwash.

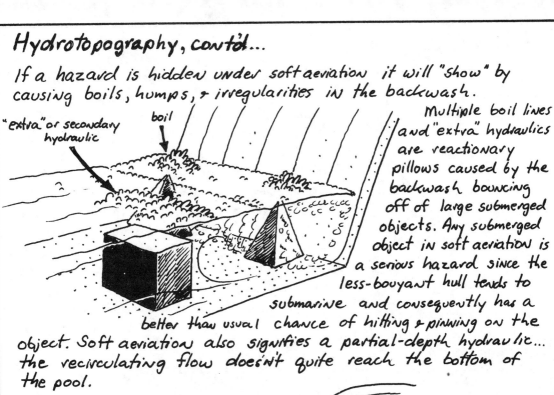

"extra" or secondary hydraulic

boil

Multiple boil lines and "extra" hydraulics are reactionary pillows caused by the backwash bouncing off of large submerged objects. Any submerged object in soft aeriation is a serious hazard since the less-bouyant hull tends to submarine and consequently has a better than usual chance of hitting & pinning on the object. Soft aeriation also signifies a partial-depth hydraulic... the recirculating flow doesn't quite reach the bottom of the pool.

Partial-depth Hydraulic

A partial-depth hole is good news for the swimmer because, down deep, there is a downstream flow to swim into. Also the swimmer won't be bounced across the bottom upon entering the downstream flow.

Where the recirculating flow extends to the bottom (full-depth hydraulic) the water ricochets off the bottom causing a less-aeriated "splashy" backwash. The air-to water ratio is low to medium. A swimmer on the downward circuit of recirculation gets bounced across the bottom, especially if he/she is trying to swim out the bottom.

Full-depth Hydraulic

oof!

Soft aeriation looks deceptively non-violent. Depending on the type of drop, it can signify a super-deadly terminal hydraulic. Below a big vertical drop in a deep pool the hydraulic will be more of an ellipse than a circle, deeper than it is wide. Unless you pencil in right on the interface chances are you won't get caught and trashed.

Soft aeriation below a big slanting drop usually means "terminal". Instead of loosing energy by diffusion in the pool below the downstream flow drives the hydraulic by friction on over half of its circumference, creating a wide powerful recirculating flow.

If you choose a line that will land you in soft aeriation, paddle hard and hit the hole with as much downstream momentum as you can summon.

On the other end of the scale we have "hard aeriation." Hard aeriation looks like water at a furious boil. Picture molten glass. The bubbles are few, big, and irregular. The air-water mix ratio is low. Hard aeriation below a big vertical drop means shallow water, irregular bottom and an irregular hydraulic. The hydraulic will kick in several different directions at once. The backwash will be splashy, violent, and freight train loud.

"Hard Aeriation"

Note extremely irregular boil line

Ka-thunk!

Never land vertical in hard aeriation coming off a big drop!

Hydrotopography, cont'd..

Medium ("Normal") aeriation — Here the air-water mix is around 50%. Medium aeriation is mainly white, splashy-gnarly, and violent. Bubbles are irregular and big (marble-size to golf ball-size). At the interface the backwash percolates and slams into the downstream flow. Medium aeriation signifies a full-depth hydraulic, uneven bottom and shallow to medium-deep water. A kayak entering medium aeriation probably won't bury completely and the kayaker can surf and brace in the backwash with relative ease. The hydraulic will be plenty powerful but a trapped boater can at least stay on top of it (unlike soft aeriation) and maintain some semblance of control. A swimmer may recirculate once or twice but he/she is sure to be blown out (via the bottom) in very short order. The Ocoee's "Hell Hole" is a good example of what I mean by medium aeriation. A western equivalent would be the big hole in Staircase Rapid on the S. Fork of the Payette River.

Mixed Aeriation — Any combination of soft, medium, and/or hard aeriation at the base of a drop signifies an uneven and possibly obstructed bottom.

Note crooked boil line

"Medium": shallow H_2O, full-depth hydraulic

"Soft": deep H_2O, partial depth hydraulic

"Hard": shallow H_2O, full-depth hydraulic

Note: Besides "hard aeriation", extremely soft splashy aeriation with multiple boils also indicates shallow water and possible unseen obstructions!

43

Hydrotopography, cont'd...

Back in the old days waterfall/big drop running style was characterized by total lack of style. We would just paddle straight off, high air brace (to keep the paddle out of our mouth when we bottomed out) and hope for the best. Macho determination substituted for skill... it was the Golden Age of Crash and Burn.

"Old Style"
Drop Running

A super-fast take-off velocity was shunned in favor of a controlled, graceful descent. It certainly _looked_ dignified...

Note: A vertical landing in a hole wherein the boat and boater submerge vertically is known as "Pencilling"

Then, one day, somewhere in Appalachia, an adrenaline-crazed creek boater ran a big drop a little too fast and something funny happened...

Ski-Jumping *
was
Born !!

Ulp!

EUREKA!

Hallelujah!
Say "Amen!

We are forever indebted to this mysterious boater, whoever he/she is...

* A.k.a. "Pancaking" out West...

44

Hydrotopography, cont'd..

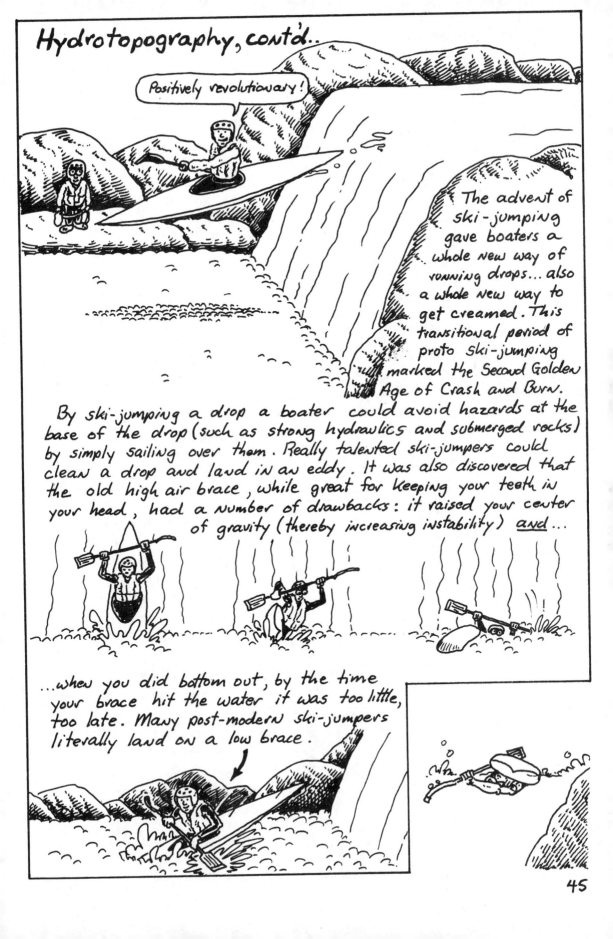

Positively revolutionary!

The advent of ski-jumping gave boaters a whole new way of running drops... also a whole new way to get creamed. This transitional period of proto ski-jumping marked the Second Golden Age of Crash and Burn.

By ski-jumping a drop a boater could avoid hazards at the base of the drop (such as strong hydraulics and submerged rocks) by simply sailing over them. Really talented ski-jumpers could clean a drop and land in an eddy. It was also discovered that the old high air brace, while great for keeping your teeth in your head, had a number of drawbacks: it raised your center of gravity (thereby increasing instability) <u>and</u>...

...when you did bottom out, by the time your brace hit the water it was too little, too late. Many post-modern ski-jumpers literally land on a low brace.

Hydrotopography, cont'd...

In order to get airborne off a drop you've got to be going FAST, at least as fast as the main current; if possible even faster. At the lip of the drop the kayaker takes a final powerful forward stroke and uses a hip thrust to shove the hull out from the face. As the boat clears the lip the back-leaning kayaker executes a dynamic "mini sit-up" to raise the bow and keep the hull as horizonal as possible. The forward stroke begun at the lip is continued on descent in a smooth, unbroken rhythm. Upon impact the opposite blade should be in position to forward sweep or brace. If a less-horizonal landing is desired the kayaker snaps forward over the bow deck just before impact.

Components of standard Ski-jump

① Preflight: final stroke begins
② Take-off: hip thrust, finish final stroke
③ In-flight: dynamic sit-up, forward stroke rhythm continues...
④ Landing: body relaxed and upright, landing gear down (ie-paddle blade is coming into position for a stroke or brace on opposite side from take-off....

Obviously, if you have 50 yards of flatwater above the drop you'll be able to get up so much take-off velocity little or no body english will be necessary. Unfortunately, that's rarely the case... most of the time you're going to be peeling out of a micro-eddy a few boat-lengths above the lip. If you can manage to get in five or six solid strokes you're lucky. Normally at least some body english will be absolutely necessary.

Hydrotopography, cont'd...

Ski-jumping is not the be all and end all of big drop-running. If you've got a nice clean drop into pleasantly aeriated deep water and a non-lethal hydraulic, why ski-jump at all? Ski-jumping can also be hazardous to your health; if you land on a rock or land flat in non-aeriated water you're going to break something (ankles, neck, back, etc.). A boat landing flat in non-aeriated water may not break the surface tension of the pool.....you may as well be landing on cement! There's a kayaker in the N.C. mountains who is an inch and a half shorter than he used to be as the result of a horizonal landing in non-aeriated water... we're talking pulverized lumbar vertebrae and some vaporized disks (ouch!).

Another hazard of ski-jumping is psychological: a boater may run a drop he/she knows is dangerous thinking he/she will merrily ski-jump to safety. In real life you may not clear the boil line, you may not miss the submerged rock. If you're using ski-jumping as a danger-avoidance technique, use it with extreme pre-judice! Ski-jumping can be done safely as long as the person in the cockpit has good judgement. Unfortunately, thats not always the case.

Hydrotopography, cont'd...

Rock-jumping – You're faced with a drop into a very terminal hydraulic. You decide that you'd as soon stick your hand into a Cuisinart as land in that hole. You notice a nice feeder eddy bottom right... the righthand rock lip is polished smooth. You decide to run diagonally, skimming off the polished lip and landing in the eddy...

..You lean forward hard after becoming airborne to insure a bow-first landing in non-aeriated water.

Skim-jumping – You're looking at some weird mixed-aeriation below a drop. Making the correct interpretation of shallow water and heavy obstruction you realize you'll pin vertically if you run the drop normally. Except for immediately below the drop the water downstream looks OK. The backwash is well-aeriated making a flat landing semi-safe. After a couple hasty prayers to the river gods you ski-jump into the unobstructed water downstream of the drop, skimming over the mixed aeriation..

Hydrotopography, cont'd...

More Skim-jumping... You're looking at an upstream vee slot with a folded flow face and a nasty hydraulic at the bottom. You assume that beneath the boiling aeriation there are some big obstructing rocks. The water just outside the "V" is medium aeriated and looks "clean". You decide to run it diagonally, starting on the bottom flow and skimming across the top flow. You hope to land just downstream of the mouth of the "V" in the clean outflow, river right...

Perhaps the best and most legitimate application of ski-jumping is running pourovers. After all, what is a pourover but a U-ledge with a super-nasty convex hole!?

49

Hydrotopography, cont'd...

Ski-jump pillow turn - You're looking at a twisting drop. It's a vertical drop into a terminal-looking hole. Below the boil line the current changes direction 90° and blasts off another drop into a so-so hole. Between the upper and lower drops, where the flow changes directions, there's a substantial non-aerated reaction pillow that guns into the bottom right edge of the bottom hole. To avoid the upper hole you plan to ski-jump into the reaction pillow, letting the left-kicking pillow turn your boat for a straight-on shot into the bottom hole...

You hit the pillow leaning way back on your stern deck to raise the bow while the pillow kicks the hull up and left. You land bracing into the pillow.

Pillows and Pressure Waves - When a fast current encounters a rock at a right angle to the rock a pillow and/or a pressure wave will result AS LONG AS THE ROCK IS NOT UNDERCUT! In fact, one of the best ways to identify an undercut rock is the lack of a pillow or pressure wave. A pressure wave will occur a short distance upstream of the obstruction while a pillow will occur against the obstruction itself...
(see next page)

pillow

pressure wave

Hydrotopography, cont'd...

While you can't really surf a pressure wave you can ferry across its upstream face and gain a little extra lateral momentum in a tight maneuvering situation...

Surfing off pillows should be done with caution! If the pillow is too aeriated or too small you can end up wrapped onto the upstream face of a rock. Stick to good-sized medium-to-hard aeriated pillows and always hit with sufficient momentum to carry you laterally past the obstruction. Just because a rock has a pillow doesn't __always__ mean it isn't undercut!

Hydrotopography, cont'd...

Any drop presents the paddler with a number of running options to choose from, depending on the desired outcome:

"Plan A" - You ski-jump diagonally left to right and land in the eddy. You fall over upon landing but you're clear of the backwash and the hole can't grab you.

"Plan B" - You ski-jump diagonally right to left and land in the backwash to the left of the main outwash. The backwash grabs your stern but you easily paddle clear of the hole.

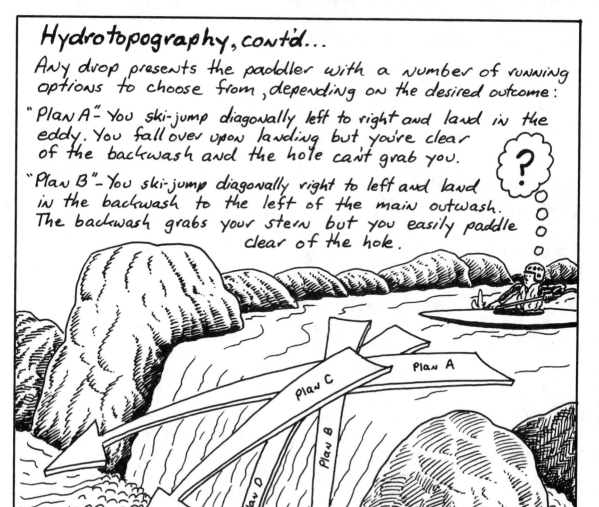

"Plan C" - You elect to ski-jump straight off the lip, intentionally landing in the main outflow. You flip on landing but the outflow kicks you clear of the backwash. You roll up...

"Plan D" - Thinking the backwash doesn't look too powerful you decide to drop straight off the lip into the maw of the hole. You bury in the soft aeration and get turned sideways in what turns out to be a very nasty hydraulic. After surfing a while you get tired and decide to go swimming. You get kicked out in the main outwash after only two recycles.

Hydrotopography, cont'd...

Hump Jumping - It's hard to "get air" going off a big slanting drop. However, you can use irregularities on the face of the drop (humps, bumps) as mini ski ramps to launch from. When contemplating a hump jump **ALWAYS** inspect your launch hump carefully... an upstream-pointing face irregularity can pin you or

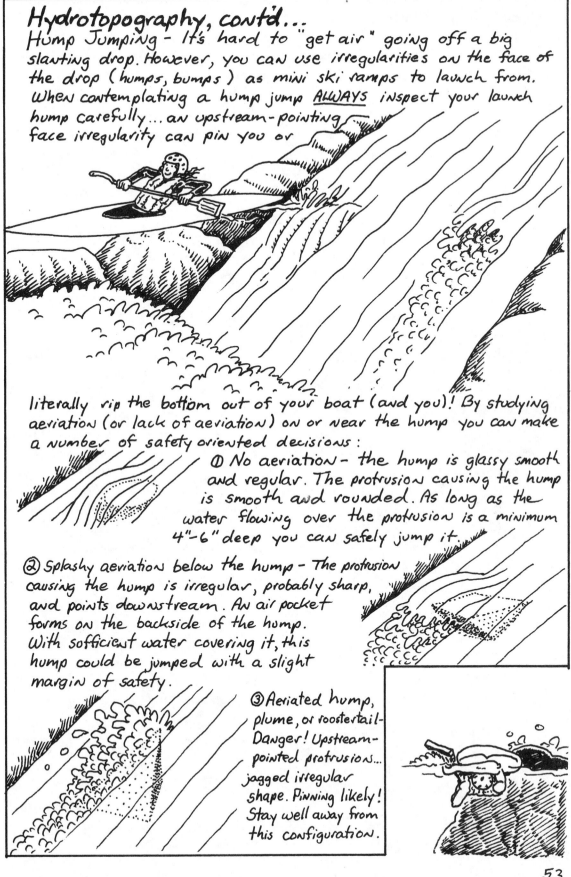

literally rip the bottom out of your boat (and you)! By studying aeviation (or lack of aeviation) on or near the hump you can make a number of safety oriented decisions:

① No aeviation - the hump is glassy smooth and regular. The protrusion causing the hump is smooth and rounded. As long as the water flowing over the protrusion is a minimum 4"-6" deep you can safely jump it.

② Splashy aeviation below the hump - The protrusion causing the hump is irregular, probably sharp, and points downstream. An air pocket forms on the backside of the hump. With sufficient water covering it, this hump could be jumped with a slight margin of safety.

③ Aeriated hump, plume, or roostertail - Danger! Upstream-pointed protrusion... jagged irregular shape. Pinning likely! Stay well away from this configuration.

Hydrotopography, cont'd...

Maneuvering on a slanting drop - When ski-jumping is impossible or undesirable you can use "plant stroke"/sweep stroke combinations to change direction on the face of the drop. Executing a "plant" on a drop is kind of like locking the brakes and twisting the steering wheel of a speeding car on a dirt road.... you're going to turn in a big hurry. For example, if you plant your paddle on your left side your boat is going to quickly pivot 180° to the left. Follow the plant with a Ninja right sweep* and you'll have made an abrupt left turn on the face of the drop.

AWK!

Ninja sweep

"Plant"

A "plant"* isn't a true stroke. To do a plant you simply jam the back face of your paddle in the water and execute a quick ½ reverse sweep. The difference between a plant and a reverse sweep is the plant begins at a right angle to your hull.... whereas the reverse sweep begins in the stern quadrant & ends in the bow quadrant. If you're moving considerably faster than the current the sweep portion of the plant becomes unnecessary - you just plant the blade and pivot 180° around a relatively stationary point.

*a.k.a "Puttin' on the brakes."

A plant is almost always followed by a fast forward sweep on the opposite side to finish the turn....

* See "Paddle Fu"

Hydrotopography, cont'd..

On irregular staircase drops (particularly really steep boulder jumbles) you can maneuver by selectively caromming off reaction pillows caused by submerged rocks. This technique can be quite hazardous if the kayaker has incorrectly read the pillows and gets pinned on a semi-submerged rock...

Hydrotopography, cont'd...

Last (but not least) of the hydrotopographical features to be discussed here are waves. Lots of boaters think that waves are only good for surfing and playing. Waves can also be used to execute dynamic maneuvers...

The Wave Crest Turn —

Wave crest turns are super-fast because so little of the hull is in contact with the water and thus has less drag. ① On the crest execute a slap stroke to stop the boat and begin pivot ② reach over the crest with your paddle and reverse sweep to turn 180°

The Dynamic Surfing Back-Ferry —

① Reverse slap-sweep on the crest.

ugh!

② reverse sweep on wave face

flow

③ etc.

④ etc.

Hydrotopography, cont'd...

The Surfing Wave Trough Turn-

On big water or flooded rivers waves come in handy for scouting...

Wave Crest Scouting-

Evasive Action

Air Traffic Control...

On steep, complex creeks and rivers, bank-scouting every drop is pretty much impractical except for the biggest drops. The probe unit can use hand signals to communicate data to those still upstream _provided_ they are conversant in the probe's hand language dialect. Caution: regional variations are common!

"Safe drop"

"Best route, line up here..."

"Move left!"

"Move right"

"Abort! Go Back"

Air Traffic Control, cont'd...

"Far left!"

"Far right!"

"Hold up for a minute..."

"Hole occupied!"

Using hand signals in lieu of scouting can be a risky proposition. <u>Never</u> run a blind drop without first scouting it! Hand signals are mainly useful for modifying what was learned during scouting. For example, the first boat through often finds a submerged rock, bad hole or undercut rock and needs to communicate this upstream.

Swimming Self Rescue

(or "Swimming lessons for those who NEVER go swimming.")

Swimming Self-rescue, cont'd...

When you go for a swim you have basically two choices; whether to float passively and hope for a rope or calm pool, or to take an active role and rescue yourself...

Passive Swimmer

Active Swimmer

If you forgot your float bags, turn the boat upsidedown to prevent further swamping

The active swimmer uses a scissor kick & one handed stroke to change position laterally in the river.

You can use the swamped boat as a surfboard of sorts...

..sit on the boat and stroke with your paddle or hands...

... or lie on the hull and stroke with your hands.

You can lie on your paddle (flat on stern deck) or push it along in front of you...

64

Swimming Self-rescue, cont'd...

Often it is best to hang onto your partially swamped boat. If you're lucky the boat will pull you under the backwash in mega-holes...

Swimming Self-rescue, cont'd...

Other uses for semi-swamped boats:

Ladder

Chock

Launching Pad

Swimming Self-rescue, cont'd...

! THUNK !

Bumper / Pivot

Not again...

Sky Hook

How to cross a strong eddyline or eddy fence:

OOF!

Swimming Self-rescue, cont'd..

You can reenter* your boat and paddle it to safety...

gasp!

*Reentry is difficult-to-impossible in anything other than a pool or slack water...

..or you can get an assist from another boater and bail your boat in the main current.

Sometimes it's best to abandon your boat and swim for it...SCREW the equipment! 'Tis a noble thing to swim your boat to shore but in a desperate situation, let it go...modern kayaks can survive pretty much anything.

Bye bye boat...

Swimming Self-rescue, contd...

Use side stroke, elementary back stroke, and crawl stroke to maneuver *when swimming rapids...

*ON a big water or flood-stage river, ditch everything and head for shore A.S.A.P. using crawl stroke!

Swimming Self-rescue, cont'd...

The Human Basketball

When swimming over big drops and/or dropping into mega-holes, tuck into a ball before you bottom out....this will protect vital areas of the body while you've being slam-dunked and subsequently bounced across the river bottom.

A well-tucked body also offers less resistance to the recirculating flow. You'll probably flush right through the hole in the deep downstream flow. If you do get recirculated, get a breath or two, tuck and try it again.

Swimming Self-rescue, cont'd..

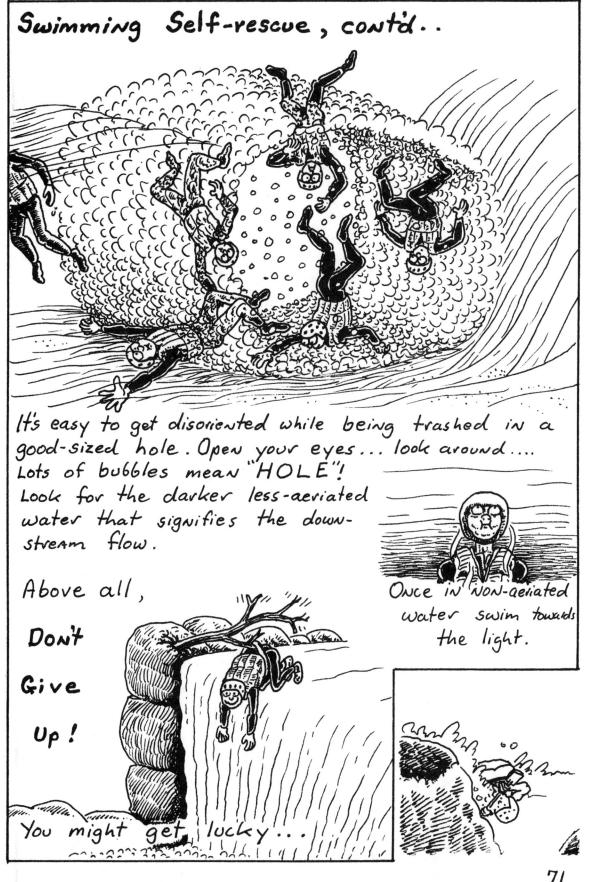

It's easy to get disoriented while being trashed in a good-sized hole. Open your eyes... look around.... Lots of bubbles mean "HOLE"! Look for the darker less-aeriated water that signifies the down-stream flow.

Once in NON-aeriated water swim towards the light.

Above all,

Don't

Give

Up!

You might get lucky...

Self Rescue
(or "Zen and the Art of Eskimo Rolling")

Self Rescue, cont'd...

The ability to consistently roll your boat in heavy water is probably the single most important skill in kayaking. There are two basic styles of rolling (low brace roll, high brace roll) and numerous refinements of the two (speed roll, hesitation roll, back roll, etc). The type of roll you choose to use is a matter of personal preference and existing river conditions.

Low Brace Roll- A fairly easy roll wherein the paddler remains tucked while rolling and ends on a low brace. Of all the roll types, the low brace roll offers the most protection to the kayaker's head and upper torso.

①

② Back hand thumb knuckle stays in contact with hull throughout the roll...

sweep

③ This roll is 90% hip snap....

④ Finish leaning forward on a low brace

Switching Sides- If you can't roll on one side, stay tucked and rotate the paddle across your helmet to the opposite side and try again...

rotate shaft here

Self Rescue, cont'd...

High Brace Roll (a.k.a. "Screw Roll") The paddler begins tucked forward and ends on a sweeping high brace leaning back over the stern deck...

front view   side view

Rotate paddle & begin sweep

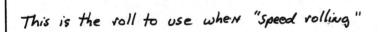

This is the roll to use when "speed rolling"

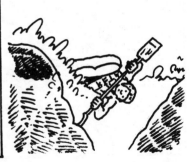

Self Rescue, cont'd...

Speed Roll (a.k.a. "Dynamic Roll"). This is a variation of the "Screw Roll". With the speed roll you intentionally (or unintentionally) capsize and roll up while maintaining your forward momentum. The speed roll is very useful in any situation where good forward motion is needed (for example: on approach to a big hole or breaking wave).

When you feel yourself getting flipped over, quickly set up to roll in the direction of the flip and go with it. Capsize vigorously and use the momentum to start coming up on the other side...

Using your capsizing momentum, begin your sweep as soon as you're fully upside down...

Instead of coming up on a brace you will be coming up on a strong forward sweep.

Bring the sweep all the way back to the stern. You should be upright and leaning back over the stern deck...

Immediately lean forward and sweep on the opposite side. If you're doing it right you should still be moving forward in a straight line when you roll up...

When speed rolling there is no hesitation between stroke-capsize-set-up-sweep and brace. It's one fluid motion and should take about three seconds to execute.

Self Rescue, cont'd...

Back Roll* – (a.k.a. "stern roll", "back-ass roll")

This difficult and awkward self-righting technique is very handy if you find yourself upside down and mashed onto your stern deck. The water is too shallow for you to risk curling forward into the tucked position preparatory to rolling...

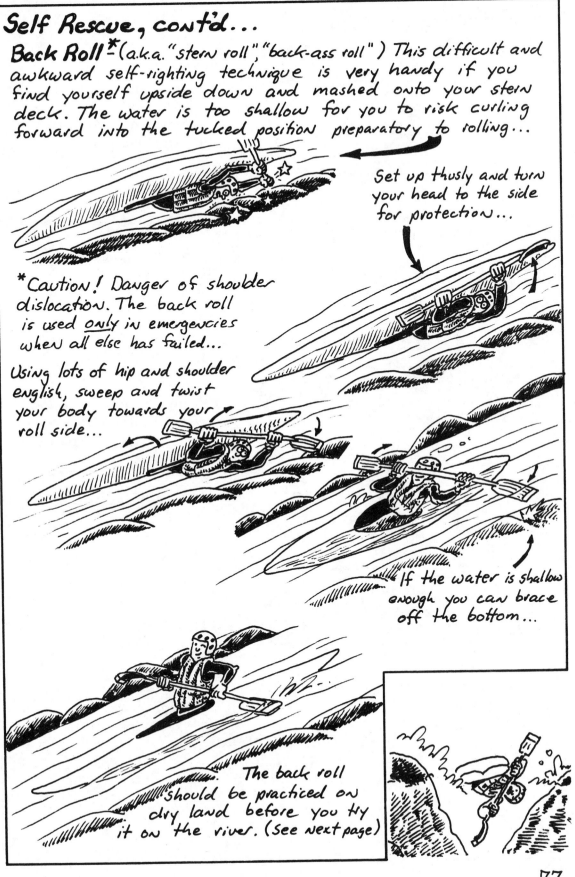

Set up thusly and turn your head to the side for protection...

*Caution! Danger of shoulder dislocation. The back roll is used only in emergencies when all else has failed...

Using lots of hip and shoulder english, sweep and twist your body towards your roll side...

If the water is shallow enough you can brace off the bottom...

The back roll should be practiced on dry land before you try it on the river. (see next page)

Self Rescue, cont'd...
Practicing the Back Roll-

① Set up in normal roll position...

② Lean all the way back onto the stern deck..

③ Flip over!

Oof!

④ Twist shoulders and hips upward and begin rotating paddle

⑤ Continue twisting and use your power blade to push yourself upright.

⑥ Finish with a strong hip-snap.

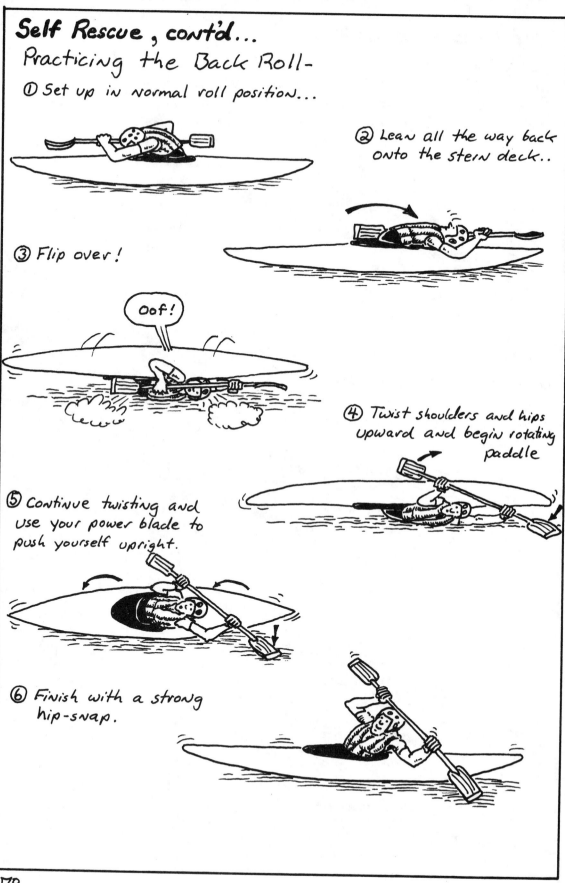

Self Rescue, cont'd...

Hesitation Roll

Hesitation Roll – The only difference between this roll and the normal eskimo roll is its rhythm. In the normal roll you set up and as soon as the power blade breaks the surface of the water you roll. With the hesitation roll you set up and wait a while, until water conditions get favorable.... then you roll. The hesitation roll is most useful in holes, wave trains, and funny water. For example, when you flip in a hole it's usually best to stay upside down until you clear the backwash. Once you hit less aeriated water (no bubbles) you roll.

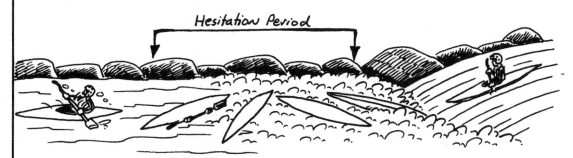
Hesitation Period

In big wave trains you want to roll up on the back side of waves so you'll be stable and ready to brace when you hit the crest...

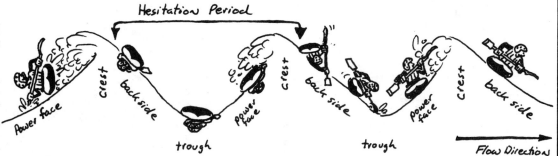
Hesitation Period

Power face — Crest — backside — trough — power face — Crest — back side — trough — power face — Crest — back side

Flow Direction

While you're hanging upside down you'll be <u>very</u> stable. If you pay attention you'll be able to feel the trough-power face-crest-back side-trough cadence of the wave train. Once you've got the timing down, wait for a crest to begin your roll. If you're lucky you'll come up on the back side where the water is slightly slower and more "solid". If you're upright by the trough, you'll be ready for the crest-breaker.

Self Rescue, cont'd...

Another advantage of hesitation rolling is you don't have to worry about rolling only on your downstream side...

If you flip in a fast current and immediately try to roll on your upstream side, the power blade will be caught by the downstream flow and pushed down... with you!

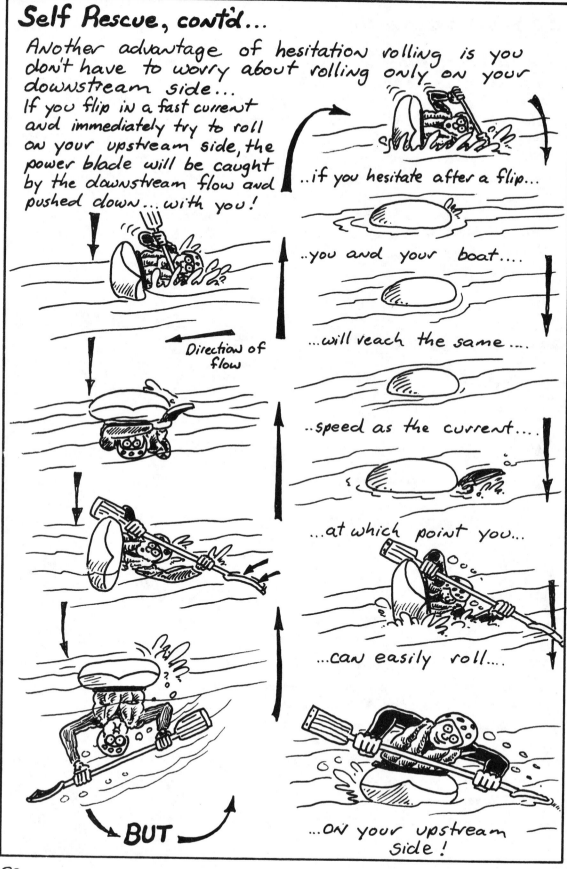

Direction of flow

..if you hesitate after a flip...

..you and your boat....

...will reach the same....

..speed as the current....

...at which point you...

...can easily roll....

...on your upstream side!

BUT

Self Rescue, cont'd...

Combat Roll

To safely paddle class III water (and up) you should develop a 100% bombproof combat roll. Whether you use a low brace roll, high brace roll, back roll, etc. (or any combination thereof) to roll up in heavy water, the trick to consistent combat rolling is pre-roll set-up. When you're upside down getting pounded by rocks is no time to have to try to figure out if you're gripping your paddle correctly, etc. I've found "anchor points" to be very helpful in combat rolling. An anchor point is a point of physical contact between you, your paddle, and your boat. Making contact with an anchor point tells you that you're in correct position under even the worst conditions. I use four anchor points: control hand, control hand thumb knuckle, off hand thumb knuckle, and lips (kissing the cockpit combing). When I'm flipped I snap forward into the tucked position and find my anchor points.... I then know I'm in the correct rolling position regardless of disorienting signals from the water around me. Then I roll... if I miss it I re-tuck and again locate the anchor points and try again. With enough practice the whole set-up/roll sequence becomes totally instinctive and automatic.

Control hand always in the same position on shaft. Placing thumb knuckle on seam line* sets the correct sweep angle on the power blade.

"Kissing the deck"- tells you that you're fully tucked & shields your head behind the power arm.

*Seam line refers to the line separating the hull from the deck.

Off hand thumb knuckle on seam line tells you the paddle shaft is "level" along the long axis of the boat.

River Rescue*

*This section is intended as a practical supplement to Bechdel & Ray's authoritative River Rescue (AMC Books, 1985). Despite what a certain geek reviewer at Canoe magazine says, it's an excellent text on advanced river rescue.
Read it!

River Rescue, cont'd...

Basic Rescue Tools:

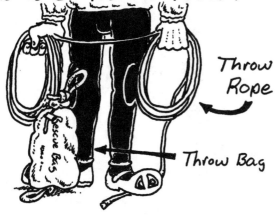

Throw Rope

Throw Bag

Brain

Chase Boat

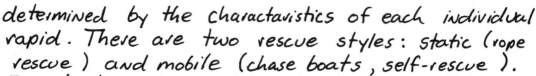

Which of these tools you choose to use should be determined by the charactaristics of each individual rapid. There are two rescue styles: static (rope rescue) and mobile (chase boats, self-rescue). Except where river conditions exclude one style or another, good boaters use a combination of the two styles. Obviously on flooded or big water rivers, rope rescue will be fairly ineffective. On steep, constricted drop-pool creeks, ropes are best to facilitate quick victim recovery, with chase boats being used strictly as a backup.

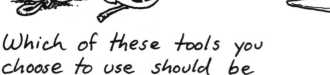

Ideal rescue set-up:

Chase boats

River Rescue, cont'd...

Boaters use ropes and chase boats on the river like a lead climber uses chocks and rope on a cliff... for protection.

Fallinnngg...

pop!

Ka-Thunk!

Always have a back-up rescue system in place in case your primary system fails...

whoa!

River Rescue, cont'd...

There are two types of rescue ropes: the throw rope (figure A) which is held in two loose coils before throwing, and the throw bag (figure B) which pays out line automatically when thrown. Without wasting ten pages discussing the relative advantages and disadvantages of the throw rope versus the throw bag, suffice it to say both types have their disadvantages. More importantly, both throw rope and throw bag require skill to use effectively so whichever type you choose to use, PRACTICE using it before you need it!

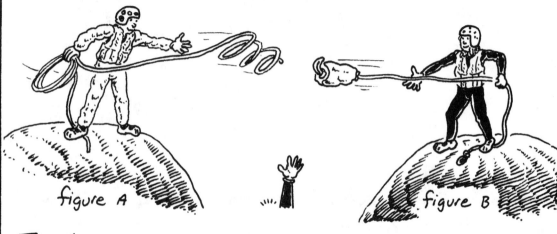

figure A

figure B

Treat your rescue rope like a climbing rope...

NO!

Stepping on the rope is a NO-NO except for anchoring purposes (one foot, near the end).

Rinse your rope after use. Sand will work its way into the braid and will weaken the rope from the inside out.

Aiieee!

Whoops..

Inspect your rope frequently. Retire and recycle worn or damaged ropes.

River Rescue, cont'd...

Rope rescue — Since the object of the game is to get the swimmer/victim to safety quickly without killing or maiming him/her in the process, the rope person should scout the rapid for hazards to avoid as well as safe spots to pull the victim into.

Undercut rock

If there is a danger of penduluming the victim into a big hole, undercut or strainer, try to find a safer spot for rescue. If there isn't a better spot, take a trial throw and measure how much rope can be thrown out and still swing in the swimmer upstream of the obstacle. Throw out that amount of rope and no more... Remember — when it's critical that the victim _not_ grab the bag, the victim _will_ grab the bag.

River Rescue, cont'd...

No matter how accurate you are with a throw bag, if you fail to anchor it properly amusing things will happen...

ROPE!

what an idiot!

Some simple anchoring methods...

You can stand on the end of the rope.

You can take a wrap around your body and hold the end in your other hand.

You can let somebody else hold the end of the rope.

NEVER tie the rope off!

River Rescue, cont'd...

...in the case of an entanglement (entrapment), a tied-off rescue rope could result in injury or death to the victim...

Tied-off objects tend to plane to the bottom!

if an entanglement occurs, release the rope immediately!

However you choose to anchor the rope, anticipate the direction of pull and position your body accordingly...

WRONG!

Aim the belay*!

*See next page

River Rescue, cont'd...

Belaying – To minimize the shock to victim and rescuer when the victim bottoms out in a fast current, the rescuer uses his/her body and/or objects (trees, rocks) to absorb the shock...
As usual, there are two styles of belaying:

① Static Belay

The rope is held tight by the rescuer, no slack is given out.

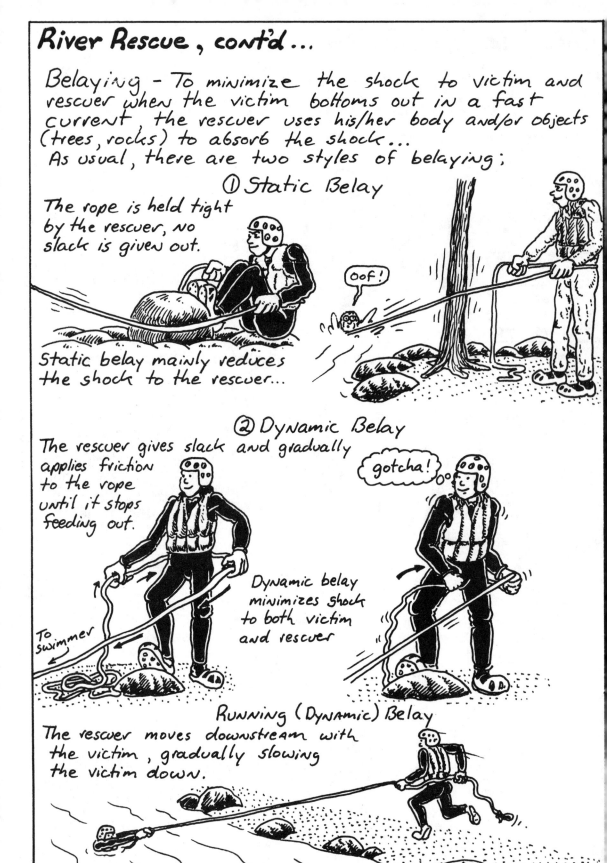

Static belay mainly reduces the shock to the rescuer...

② Dynamic Belay

The rescuer gives slack and gradually applies friction to the rope until it stops feeding out.

Dynamic belay minimizes shock to both victim and rescuer

To swimmer

Running (Dynamic) Belay

The rescuer moves downstream with the victim, gradually slowing the victim down.

River Rescue, cont'd...

How to get a stranded swimmer to shore with a significant hazard downstream:

Rope person Ⓐ sets up belay for a pendulum. Chase boater takes the rescue rope to the victim Ⓑ.

Rope person Ⓐ uses static belay to pendulum victim Ⓑ across channel to Ⓒ. The chase boater ferrys back across with the victim in case the pendulum fails.

An alternative to the pendulum is the "dynamic body surf" wherein two rope persons literally jerk the victim across the channel. If the victim manages to hang on, he/she will hydroplane into the shore...

River Rescue, cont'd ...

Rope Tricks: **The Dülfer Wrap**

The Dülfer wrap is how early mountaineers did their rappelling. It's easy to learn, requires no extra equipment (such as carabiners, brake-bars, figure 8's, seat slings, etc.) and can be set up very quickly. Used on a cliff, it hurts like hell (unless you use an elaborate padding system) which explains why early mountaineers were such excellent down-climbers.

Besides hair portaging, the Dülfer can be used in horizonal modes (see following page). Practice Dülfering on moderate inclines before you try it on a cliff!

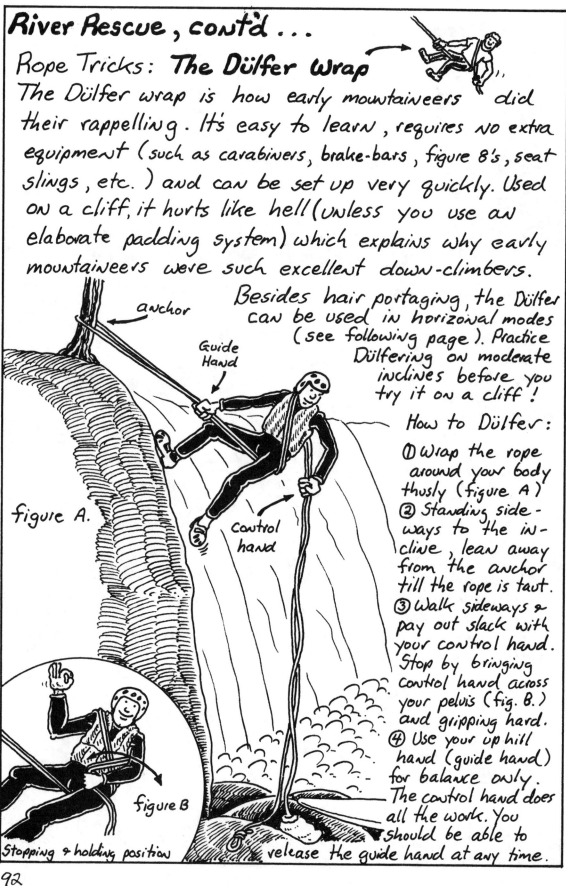

anchor

Guide Hand

figure A.

Control hand

figure B

Stopping & holding position

How to Dülfer:

① Wrap the rope around your body thusly (figure A)

② Standing sideways to the incline, lean away from the anchor till the rope is taut.

③ Walk sideways & pay out slack with your control hand. Stop by bringing control hand across your pelvis (fig. B.) and gripping hard.

④ Use your up hill hand (guide hand) for balance only. The control hand does all the work. You should be able to release the guide hand at any time.

River Rescue, cont'd...

The Dülfer is great for getting to entrapment victims, stranded equipment, and injured boaters... _if_ you're short-handed. Caution: Do not attempt Dülfer lowering in water more than waist deep!!

Once you reach the victim, hold yourself in place with your control hand and work with your guide hand

...if you get in trouble, tuck your chin and use your guide hand to flip rope over your head.

River Rescue, cont'd...

Rope Tricks: How to get a stranded boater off the river without a swim...

River Rescue, cont'd...

Rope Tricks – Dynamic Tow

This is used for fast boat-to-boat hydraulic extractions. The rescuer pops his/her sprayskirt, grabs the throw bag, re-seals the sprayskirt and throws the rope to the victim...

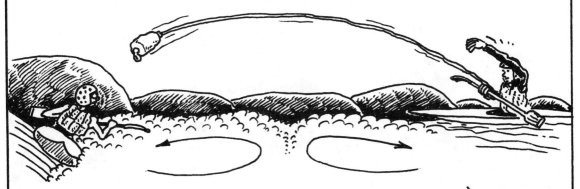

..the victim grabs the rope (see page 97), secures it and hangs on. The rescuer peels out into the downstream flow and lets the current tow the victim out of the hole.

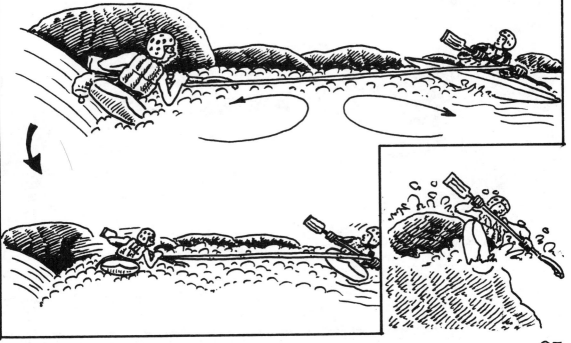

River Rescue, cont'd...

Assorted Rope Tricks :

One rope person can safely belay a rescue boat for a hole extraction rescue under two conditions: ① If the rope person can find a place to sit or stand directly downstream of the hole, and ② if the end knot is removed from the rescue rope. If the end knot isn't removed it will snag in the grab loop causing a possible entanglement.

The rope is passed through the stern grab loop and is paid out by the rope person. If the rescue boat gets sucked into the hole and can't be pulled out, the rope person pulls the rope out of the grab loop. The rope is then used as a throw rope...

River Rescue, cont'd...

The One-handed Side-surf, or how to catch a rope in a hole...

With your upstream arm reach over the paddle shaft & grab the rope while keeping the shaft secured with your upper arm pressing into your chest

Slide your arm back across the paddle shaft & with rope in hand, grasp the shaft

Lean away from the rope and hipsnap to your upstream side to stay upright.

River Rescue, cont'd...

Here's what happens if you ① grab the rope with both hands, and/or ② fail to use correct body english (upstream lean, upstream hipsnap)

Correct method

The combination of upstream lean and upstream hipsnap causes the hull to plane over the backwash.

River Rescue, cont'd...

If it becomes obvious you and your boat won't be coming out together, you'll want to bail out semi-upright while still holding onto the rescue rope...

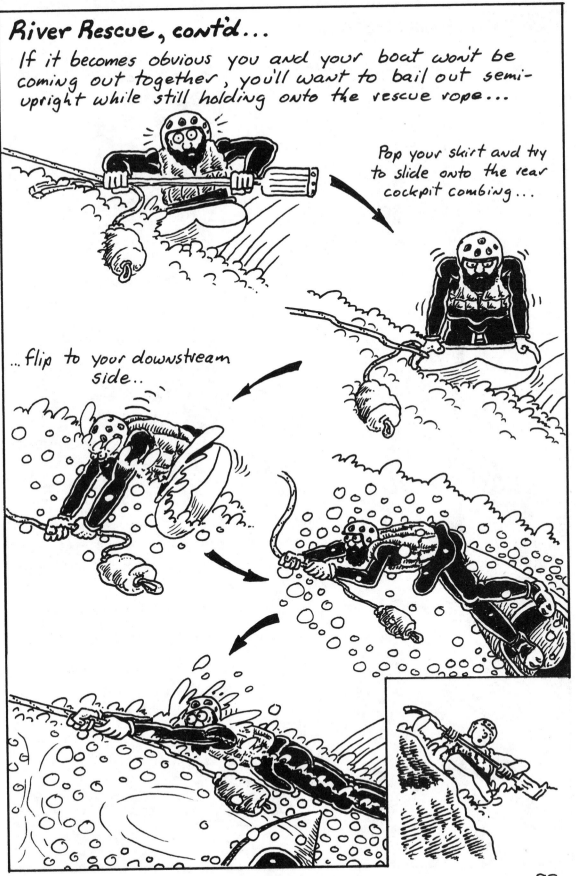

Pop your skirt and try to slide onto the rear cockpit combing...

...flip to your downstream side...

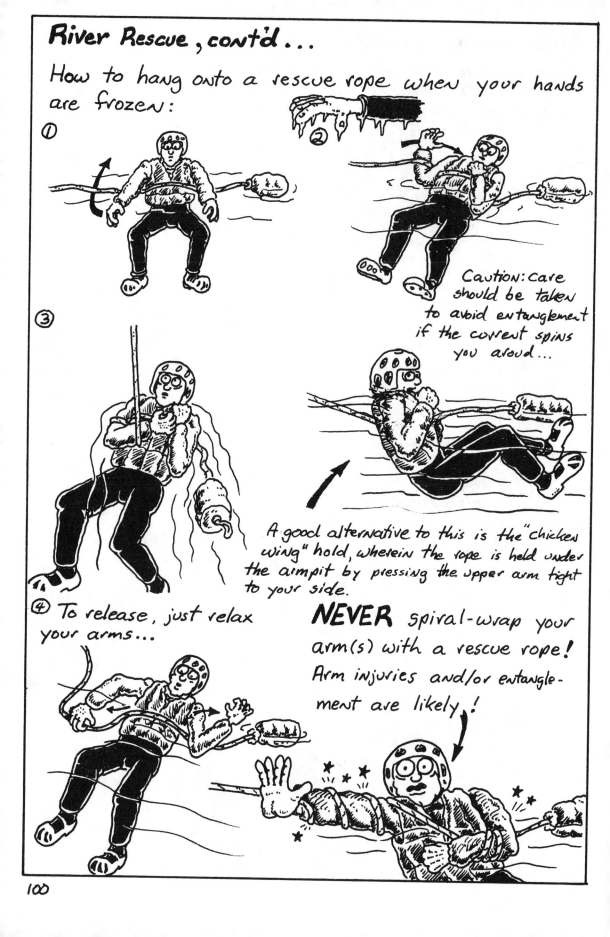

River Rescue, cont'd...

How to hang onto a rescue rope when your hands are frozen:

①

②

Caution: care should be taken to avoid entanglement if the current spins you around...

③

A good alternative to this is the "chicken wing" hold, wherein the rope is held under the armpit by pressing the upper arm tight to your side.

④ To release, just relax your arms...

NEVER spiral-wrap your arm(s) with a rescue rope! Arm injuries and/or entanglement are likely!

River Rescue, cont'd...

When you are faced with a semiconcious or unconcious victim it's time to go swimming... fast! Ideally another chase boat will be available to assist the swimming rescuer and victim...

The object of the game here is to get the victim's head out of the water, get to shore, and give life support...

River Rescue, cont'd...
Chase Boating

This exciting sub-sport of kayaking involves running dangerous rapids while in pursuit of or while actually towing fear-crazed victims. Born in the Southeast, chase boating began as a way to atone for leaving your rescue rope in the car. Since the early days, chase boating has evolved into a complex and beautiful Artform, a "ballet of catastrophe" if you will. Today, chase boating and rope tossing have combined to form a virtually bomb-proof method for extricating hapless boaters from the rivers and creeks they've fallen into. Modern chase boat technique is governed by:

The Top Three Commandments

1. Thou shalt not, by thy efforts, put Thyself and thy swimmer in more danger than the swimmer was in originally. (Doctrine of Extra Danger)

River Rescue, cont'd...

2. Thou shalt never make physical contact with any swimmer until Thou hast ascertained the mental state of that same swimmer. (Doctrine of Presumed Insanity)

mfft... rrgh!

3. Verily, the Chase Boater is like as a god, and the swimmer but a wretched supplicant unto Him/Her. As the naughty dog fears its angry master, so shall the miscreant swimmer fear the wrath of the Chase Boater if His/Her every command is not instantly obeyed. (Doctrine of Supreme Ascendancy of Chase Boaters)

Victim Behavior...

Help me, O Great One. I beg you... please....

Wrong!

Right!

Sooner or later, every chase boater will screw up and make contact with one of the living dead. The chase boater will be dragged into holes, off waterfalls, and/or into strainers. The swimmer will climb onto the chase boater's head using his/her paddle as a ladder. Learn how to recognize the bad victim and avoid him (or her)!

River Rescue, con'td...

For the chase boater, there are two kinds of victim..

Good Victim

Bad Victim

Bad victims are usually raft customers or tandem canoeists. Infrequently they are kayakers, but if they are, they are beginners. Bad Victim symptoms include: barking (arf! rarf!), flailing limbs, inability to speak multisyllable words, moaning, yelling, etc. The best way to tell if a kayaker is freaked out is if he/she _doesn't_ say "I'm OK... get my boat!". Once the bad victim is identified, keep a prudent distance and offer verbal support....tell them a joke. This will take his/her mind off what's fixing to happen. If the victim calms down you can explain how you _might_ assist him/her _if_ he/she remains calm and rational.

How to dislodge a bad victim:

River Rescue, cont'd...

The chase boat has four primary functions:

① Psychological Support

...so the salesman says to the farmer...

② Rescue Platform

③ Tow Truck

puff...

④ Bulldozer

Before contact with the victim is made, the chase boater evaluates the physical situation and comes up with THE PLAN. Given the fluid dynamics of the river environment, THE PLAN will probably change during the actual rescue, but it _does_ provide the rescuer and victim with a framework to operate in. Besides, coming up with THE PLAN gives the chase boater something to do besides surfing and getting enders...

The chase boater should prescout the area downstream prior to rescue.

River Rescue, cont'd

Chase boaters usually operate in pairs, one taking the swimmer, the other the boat and miscellaneous equipment. The reason for this labor division is simple; towing a boater _and_ a swamped boat is virtually impossible in heavy water. Equipment is always considered secondary until the victim is adequately protected by at least one chase boat...

To reduce drag of feet and legs of victim you can put him/her under your bow with arms & legs wrapped over your deck. It looks pretty kinky but it works!

The chase boat towing the victim has three options:
① Tow the victim straight to shore.
② Run the rapid with the victim and eddy out at the bottom.

③ Set the victim up for a safer swim...

good luck!

River Rescue, cont'd...

Actual towing of swimmers is, on average, a slow exhausting experience. Don't be shy about ordering the victim to kick to assist you, since most victims will simply hang on like a remora on a shark (if you're not an ichthyologist read "useless appendage") until given verbal inducement...

Since you're not gonna kick, do you have any last words?

gulp!

You can take some of the effort out of towing by using the main current to gain speed then blasting through an eddyline from upstream...

Whether to tow the victim from the bow or stern is a matter of personal preference and overall river conditions. It's easier to maneuver the bow grabloop to the victim in heavy water but towing is made harder if the victim is on the bow. You can let the victim move hand-over-hand from bow to stern (or vice versa) as conditions vary..

Put suspected bad victims on the bow loop so you can keep an eye on them!

River Rescue, cont'd...

In a situation where the chase boater has to get the victim across an eddy fence, other members of the party can set up a human-boat chain for the victim to grab from the eddy perimeter...

Most of the time when a swimmer hits an eddy fence he/she will be sucked under and carried some distance downstream before reappearing on or near the eddy line...

...if a chase boater looses his/her victim in the eddy fence, the chase boater should continue downstream at main flow speed on the eddy line and wait for the victim to resurface.

River Rescue, cont'd...

Many swimmers have a tendency to let go of the grab loop too soon upon entering an eddy, thinking they can swim for it. The chase boater should make it clear to the swimmer to hang on until the chase boater says "Let go". (Premature Disconnection Syndrome)

This will avoid the chase boater having to perform two rescues...

If you have a swimmer being recirculated in a hole you can sit just below the boil line and catch the swimmer when he/she bobs up. Don't try this on any hole you wouldn't be willing to surf because there's a chance the victim will pull you into the hole with him/her.

Offering your bow loop is easiest because you can position yourself better in relation to the victim and the boil line if you can see well...

The Joy of
Flood

(or "Big water technique-
-if-you-subtract- the-trees-
and-debris.")

The Joy of Flood...

Introduction

Each Spring we get a big rain followed by a beautiful sunny day. We load up the boats and head down to the local river which is running at or above floodstage levels. Every time there is a big group of idiots at the put in unloading 'surplus' rafts and/or rented canoes. We ask them not to run. We explain the dangers of flood and tell them that they'll probably drown within sight of the put in. Common sense and logic. It never works, we've only gotten their test-tosterone flowing better. When the truth fails...lie! Here are some lines that work:

① "Before you go, could you please give us the name and number of someone to call to identify your remains?"

② "There's a farmer with a shotgun just around the bend waiting for you. The river is so far out of its banks he'll shoot you for trespassing!"

③ "The last guys they hauled out of here in a helicopter had to pay $5,000 <u>each</u> for the rescue!"

④ "Every water moccasin in that river is gonna climb into that raft with you and be on you like a pit bull on Granny!"

The snake one never fails. After they leave we run the river. Now I'm not advocating flood paddling. But lots of us run flood, either by accident (flash flood), misadventure (ignorance of river level) or choice (defective genetic programming).

The Joy of Flood, con'td...

If you were to ask me "Mr. Nealy, I'm an expert. Should I paddle flooded rivers?" I would say "No. But if you do, you should read this and learn from my mistakes." So, right or wrong, here is what I know:

First of all we should recognize that running flooded rivers is, at best, an unsafe activity. So is driving. Floodstage boating demands expert-level paddling skills, absolutely bomb-proof self-rescue skills, good to excellent rescue skills, extra-ordinary river-reading skills (from the cockpit), prior experience on and good working knowledge of the river being paddled, a cool head, and a cavalier attitude. Prior knowledge of the river is the most important of these preconditions. If you don't already know the river, <u>do</u> <u>not</u> attempt to paddle it at flood!! At floodstage, deadly and unavoidable hazards (riverwide hydraulics, log-jams, bridges, etc) are very likely. Your prior knowledge of what lies downstream will largely determine if you are to survive the experience. If you don't know where the mega-holes, strainers, and exploding waves are likely to be, you'll end up fish food. Be careful out there. And remember what the bad boys say, "If you can't do the time, don't do the crime."

ulp!

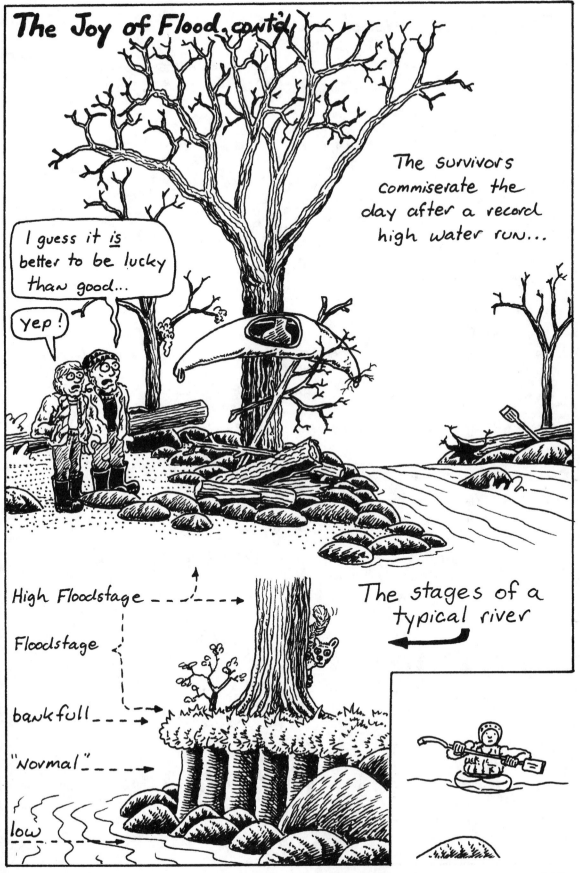

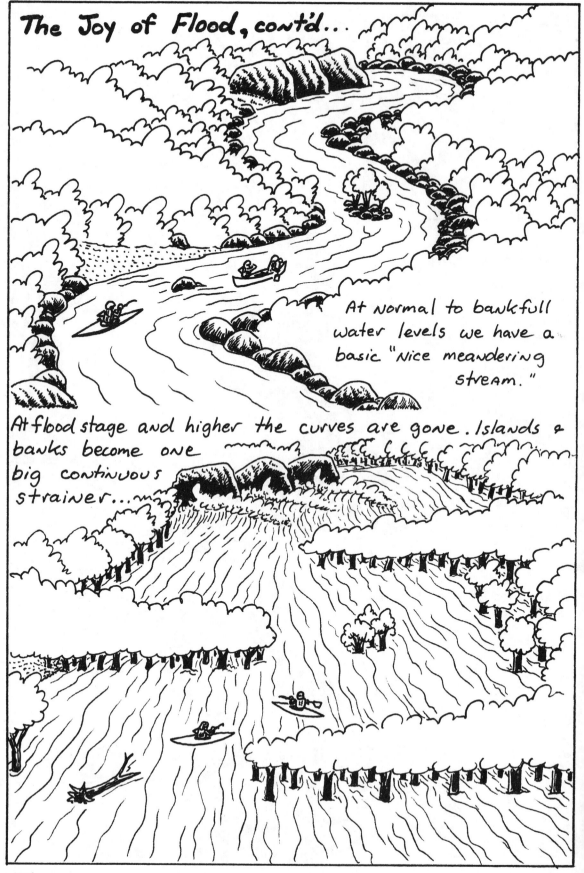

The Joy of Flood, cont'd...

At normal to bankfull water levels we have a basic "nice meandering stream."

At flood stage and higher the curves are gone. Islands & banks become one big continuous strainer...

The Joy of Flood, cont'd...

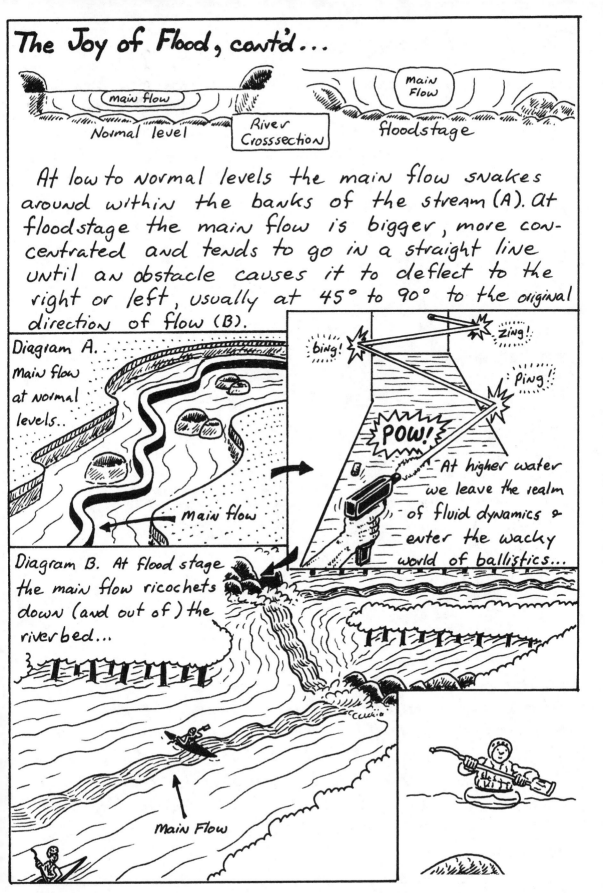

main flow

Normal level

River Crosssection

Main Flow

floodstage

At low to normal levels the main flow snakes around within the banks of the stream (A). At floodstage the main flow is bigger, more concentrated and tends to go in a straight line until an obstacle causes it to deflect to the right or left, usually at 45° to 90° to the original direction of flow (B).

Diagram A. Main flow at normal levels.

Main flow

bing!

Zing!

Ping!

POW!

At higher water we leave the realm of fluid dynamics & enter the wacky world of ballistics...

Diagram B. At flood stage the main flow ricochets down (and out of) the riverbed...

Main Flow

The Joy of Flood, cont'd...

When the main flow changes direction suddenly there will be a "Zone of Funny Water" just opposite the new direction of flow. Depending on water depth and current velocity the funny water can be exploding reaction waves, a powerful eddy fence, or a whirlpool. Or all three at once...

The Zone of Funny Water is difficult to see from upstream. However, you can recognize favorable conditions and anticipate it with the appropriate braces or avoid it completely. In the diagram above the boater in the white boat stayed center and blindly floated into the eddy fence where crosscurrents trashed him & sucked him out of his boat. The boater in the dark boat anticipated the Z.F.W. and moved far left accordingly.

The Joy of Flood, contd...

Conventional kayak wisdom would say to approach this curve hugging the inside of the turn (right). Unfortunately this puts the boater into a major Zone of Funny Water. 'Tis far better to stay in the main flow and surf the reaction waves...

The safest route (dotted line) would be just outside the eddy fence, just right of center.

zone of funny water

If there do happen to be any strainers on the outside of the turn you should be able to spot them in time to take evasive action by quickly surfing toward the inside of the curve.

Awk!

The Joy of Flood, cont'd...

Look at the river, somewhere out there is the main flow;

main Flow

Another river cross-section: relative water velocity;

Main Flow

moderate to fast | fast | Very Fast (screaming) | fast | moderate to fast

It's important to know exactly where the main flow is because...

Where wide hydraulics are concerned, this is the most likely place for a break in the hole...

Unfortunately, if the hole isn't broken by the main flow, this will be the worst part of the hole!

In slower water (dynamic pools) the main flow will be bounded by funny water...

This is where you <u>don't</u> want to be when swimming.

The Joy of Flood, cont'd...

Other flood-related peculiarities...

Low Head Dams become 100% fatal

A swimmer in the water for 4 minutes will be flushed $1\frac{1}{2}$ to 2 miles...

The rapid it took you 20 minutes to bank scout takes about 5 seconds to run...

Some rapids disappear ("wash out") and new ones appear in surprising places...

Once in a rapid, downstream visibility becomes practically zero...

Individual rapids connect and form one long Mega-Rapid...

The Joy of Flood, cont'd...

Flood Style: Paddling fast downstream doesn't make a lot of sense, seeing as you are already being conveyed downstream at a brisk 12-20+ mph. You need to go slow so you can do a little wave-crest scouting. While Walt Blackadar advocated passive sideways or backward floating in heavy water, a passive-aggressive approach is better...

Either Sideways

Or Backwards

Use fast downstream paddling selectively to punch holes and breaking waves as well as for threading your way between them.

You can use small holes as eddies for scouting or resting...

The Joy of Flood, cont'd...

..No matter how good you & your party think you are, sooner or later someone is going to go swimming..

unless there's a killer rapid coming up it's preferable to keep the swimmer in the main flow until a "safe" calm spot can be found to get the swimmer out.

.. or the swimmer can re-enter his/her boat, bail and continue.

...sometimes the swimmer is forced to grab a tree and work toward the bank...

The Joy of Flood, cont'd...

Here's one way to get a good idea of the forces involved in contacting trees in fast-moving water...

① Get on your mountain bike (or equivalent) and get moving at about 15-20 miles per hour...

Wear your gloves!

② Select a suitable tree (preferably one surrounded by soft grassy turf.)

③ Grab the tree as you pass by...

Oof!

④ Conclusion: avoid contact with trees in fast-moving water whenever possible!

The Joy of Flood, cont'd..

Most of the time you will assume "The Position" and use your feet to push away from trees and other obstacles...

"The Position"

Chorus: Stay away from trees in moving water!

Aargh!

BUT...sometimes you need to grab a tree (to avoid a strainer, for instance). Grab the tree as you're passing to the side and swing around to the downstream side. Use the eddy there to dodge the current...

OOF!

NEVER try to grab a tree from its upstream side!!

The Joy of Flood, contd..

Some other flood-related hazards you are likely to encounter:

mobile strainers

Barbed Wire

Low-water bridges

High-water bridges

Dead livestock

Whirlpools

The Joy of Flood, cont'd...

Q: So... given the vast number of objective hazards associated with floodstage river-running (trees, strainers, mega-holes, whirlpools, funny water, exploding waves, etc., etc.) __why do__ we run flooded rivers?

A: Because it's fun.

Floodstage paddling is like riding on top of a runaway freight train on a steep mountain grade.

First Aid for Riverrunners

Take a First Aid Course !!

The skills necessary for emergency wilderness life support cannot be learned by reading a book. Suggested courses: Advanced First Aid – American Red Cross; Lifesaving – American Red Cross; Cardio pulmonary Resuscitation and Advanced Life Support – American Heart Association; and/or any EMT course.

Another true whitewater tale of terror...

Your Notes

Begin Animation

Appendix

(reprinted from *Whitewater Home Companion*, Volume II

Survival ...Holes and Breaking Waves —

How to get munched....

Paddler enters hole with no extra downstream momentum, sitting upright and air bracing...
fig 1

Boat catches stern in downstream current when bow is lifted by the hole's upstream flow. Upright upper torso acts as water-scoop to further impede downstream progress...

fig 2

...boat slips backwards into maw of hole and boater executes an inverted high brace...

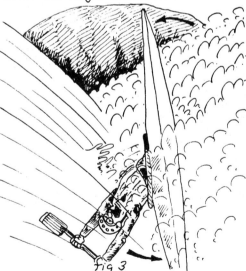

fig 3

...after a good thrashing, boater decides to take his chances body-surfing the hole.

fig 4

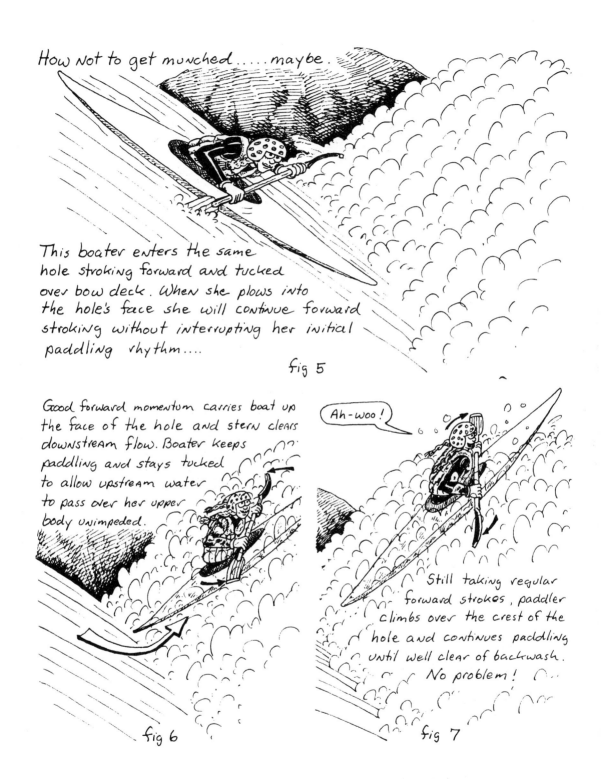

How not to get munched.....maybe.

This boater enters the same hole stroking forward and tucked over bow deck. When she plows into the hole's face she will continue forward stroking without interrupting her initial paddling rhythm....

fig 5

Good forward momentum carries boat up the face of the hole and stern clears downstream flow. Boater keeps paddling and stays tucked to allow upstream water to pass over her upper body unimpeded.

fig 6

Ah-woo!

Still taking regular forward strokes, paddler climbs over the crest of the hole and continues paddling until well clear of backwash. No problem!

fig 7

Switching the Lead....

g-g-g-god!

Often a boater will enter a rapid first and come to the frightening realization that ① he/she is totally out of control & disoriented and/or ② his/her initial appraisal of the diff- iculty of the rapid was incorrect and he/she is about to get munched...

Not wanting his/her paddling buddies to think he/she is a wimp the boater must somehow switch the lead while making it appear unintentional. You can make certain physical laws work for you......

1st Law - When two or more boats occupy a micro-eddy, the first boat in the eddy will be the last to leave.

All you have to do is find a tiny eddy and trick someone into joining you in it...

Ender spot!

Whew!

fait accompli!

2nd Law – Sponge-bailing a decked boat in a class Ⅳ rapid is a necessary but time-consuming process.

Pop your skirt in the first available eddy and bail furiously while the others pass.

3rd Law – A photographer ideally should be first into a rapid and the last out in order to fully capture the excitement of the moment on film...

Your friends will gladly probe the nasty stuff for you as long as you immortalize them on slide film. They will also rescue you first....

4th Law – Surfing is a more noble endeavor than leading and thus always takes precedence over leading.....

Jump on the first wave you see and find out how long you can surf it. Your friends will get bored watching you and proceed downstream.

5th Law – A loose footbrace or thigh-strap must be readjusted at the first opportunity in the interest of group safety...

It's that damned footbrace again!

Reading Boaters...

On really steep creeks and rivers, bank-scouting is nearly impossible and blind drops leave no upstream signature. Thus the prudent boater will learn to carefully observe the leader (or "probe") for physical cues that may indicate danger below...

However, it's what happens to the probe after the drop that really matters...

A loud bumping noise, screams and an immobile stern usually indicate a bad pinning spot!

Furious backpaddling at the edge of a drop may indicate bad news below...

Any unusually long disappearance of the probe is a good indication of a keeper hydraulic....

Whichever side the probe washes out on is probably the safest route through the hydraulic...

Best Route

Significant lateral displacement of the probe means powerful cross-currents just below !

Probe's final trajectory

displacement

Probe's initial trajectory

This suggests a hard brace on your left side !

A backendeved probe probably means a powerful but deep hole just below...

You can probably ski-jump the worst of it

Total destruction of the probe indicates a mandatory portage !

Ulp!

Eddies, Eddy Walls, Interfaces...

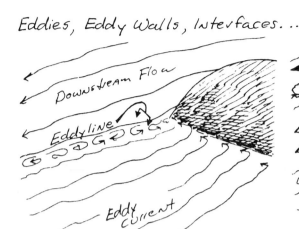

At any water level, an eddyline is the interface of the fast-moving downstream flow and the slower upstream eddy flow.

Leave the eddy pointed upstream... a downstream lean and solid low brace will keep the eddy-line "user friendly."

At high water levels the eddy-line transforms into a powerful hydraulic-like eddy-wall.....

Super-depressed eddies are the most common. The eddy is lower than the main current...

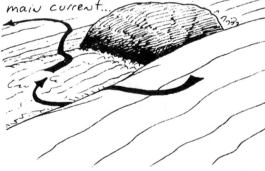

A superelevated eddy bulges higher than the main flow. The boater must punch the "wall" and climb onto the eddy. This type of eddy is usually found below pourovers....

You enter a super-depressed eddy by literally dropping into it. To paddle out you must punch the eddy wall and climb up onto the main flow. Needless to say, these are **squirrelly places to be.**

Whether the high-water eddy is super-elevated or super-depressed the approach to entering and exiting are pretty much the same. Pretend the eddy wall/interface is a hole and act accordingly...

To enter a superelevated eddy, enter pointed downstream, punch the wall, brace and keep paddling until you're well clear of the interface

Enter a superdepressed eddy on an upstream ferry

Exit the eddy pointed upstream with lots of forward momentum. After you hit the main flow maintain a good upstream ferry angle and paddle well beyond the interface before peeling downstream.

If you try to peel on the interface itself you get eaten....

To exit, establish a good upstream ferry angle and start paddling from the bottom of the eddy. Punch the wall and continue ferrying out well beyond the interface before peeling downstream.

At floodstage, what used to be big deep pools often become whirlpools, particularly pools with an obstruction on the downstream side.

A swimmer or boater caught in such an "eddy" will be recirculated along A-B-C-D indefinately.....

The main ways to judge the relative seriousness of a whirlpool-eddy are ① Is there blockage on the downstream end of the eddy? ② Is the eddy full of debris; logs, milk jugs, etc moving in a spiral? If "yes" to either or both questions stay away!

Like a rescue from a hydraulic, the object is to pull the victim out without putting the rescuers in the same predicament....

Logs and trees caught in the whirlpool pose additional danger for both victim and rescuer....

Entering the whirlpool for a boat rescue has another drawback....

recrossing the interface with victim in tow can cause you to flip when the interface current grabs the victim and sucks him under.

For a successful boat rescue you've got to cross the interface at its weakest point, usually at the downstream end. The best way is to rescue the victim from shore as he's being recirculated (C or D). From shore use paddle or short length of rope to reach victim.

The swimmer will be sucked down at the upstream end of the interface & will pop up a ways downstream on the interface. If your stern is in place when victim resurfaces you can probably pull him out....

Frequently a swimmer will be pulled into an interface by rescuers using ropes. Rescuers should read the interface and decide whether it is safe to pull a swimmer across an interface and into an eddy or to swing the swimmer into shore below the eddy......

Rescuer B swings the swimmer into shore below the whirlpool. Rescuer C grabs the victim before he is swept upstream and ultimately back into the interface.

Rescuer A is positioned at the top of the eddy and pendulums the victim into the worst part of the interface. Victim lets go of rope.....

141

High Brace vs. Low Brace; the debate continues...

Which is better?

High Brace

Low Brace

If you flip downstream...

High brace - a sudden flip can result in hyperextension of the shoulder joint.....dislocation!

Low brace - quickly tuck into roll position and get oriented...

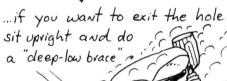

...even if you didn't dislocate your shoulder you'll find getting into roll position can result in a human pretzel..

...if you want to exit the hole sit upright and do a "deep-low brace"

...to roll up, sweep and hipsnap....
end on a low brace!

Meanwhile, our high bracer decides
to swim for it and seek medical
attention.....

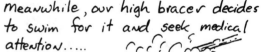

Possibly the best way to achieve traumatic dislocation is to drop into a
big hole sideways in a high brace position....

Combined
energy of hole
and paddler
absorbed here!

fig 1.

boat stops
here

paddle tends
to stay near
the crest of
the hole...

rriiiippp!

fig 2.

...the low brace position, however, is a complex suspension system
with wrist, elbow, shoulder, and hips acting as shock absorbers...

fig 3.

Energy is absorbed
and dissipated over
a wide area!

fig 4.

Here's an experiment you can do at home....

① Take a 3' length of ⅜" polypropylene rope; tie one end to a door knob and hold the other end firmly clamped between your teeth. Sitting 3' from jamb, open door 18".... this is a low brace simulator. (see ②)?

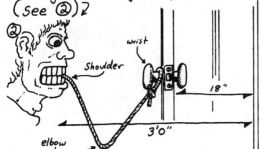

③ Have assistant kick the door closed. Notice teeth remain in mouth.

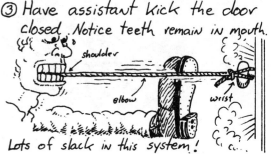

Lots of slack in this system!

Now open door 18" and move chair 18" further back - this is a high brace simulator. The taut rope represents a fully extended downstream arm in the high brace position. The 18" space between knob and jamb represents the paddler's downstream momentum and your assistant's foot represents the energy of the hole....

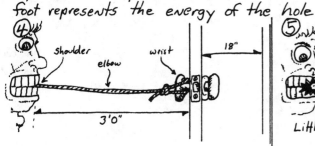

urk!

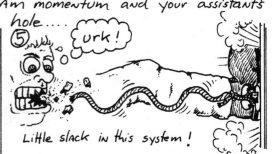

Little slack in this system!

As you can readily see, the high brace position has insufficient slack to absorb the energy of moving paddler and hole. The low brace system had slack to spare!

Q; Which is safer? ⓐ low bracing or ⓑ high bracing?

Low Brace
Simulator
Results

Answer - "a."

High Brace
Simulator
Results

Another excellent way to dislocate your shoulder is to attempt to high brace upstream on an upstream flip.....

Simultaneously, paddler hits head and paddle on rock. *And* dislocates shoulder.

In the same situation, if you're already low bracing, pivot upstream, tuck and use your falling momentum to roll up.....

①

② Head and paddle clear submerged Rock.

③ Begin sweep and hipsnap when your upper body hits aeriated water

④ End on a low brace.

Power Rolling!

One more method to achieve dislocation - trying to pull the boat out of a hole on a high brace....

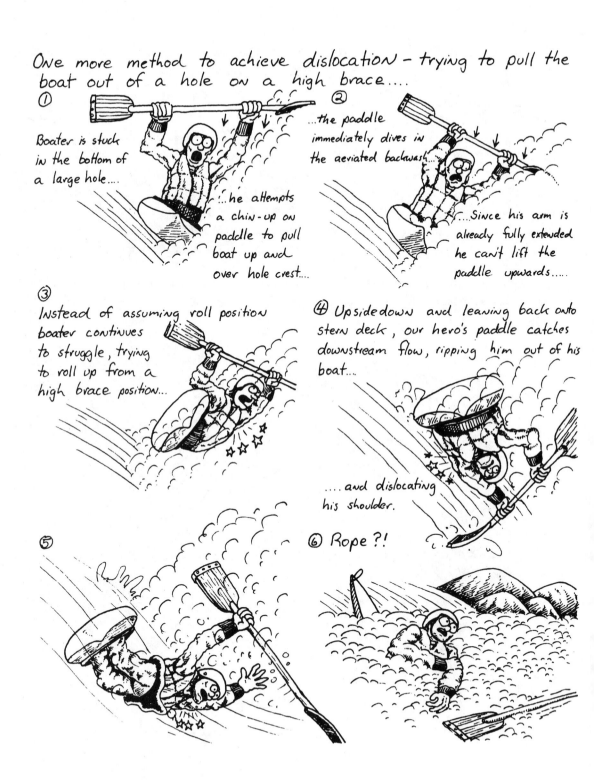

① Boater is stuck in the bottom of a large hole....

...he attempts a chin-up on paddle to pull boat up and over hole crest....

② ...the paddle immediately dives in the aeriated backwash...

...Since his arm is already fully extended he can't lift the paddle upwards.....

③ Instead of assuming roll position boater continues to struggle, trying to roll up from a high brace position...

④ Upsidedown and leaning back onto stern deck, our hero's paddle catches downstream flow, ripping him out of his boat...

....and dislocating his shoulder.

⑤

⑥ Rope?!

The low bracer uses reverse sweeps, back braces, and foreward sweeps to surf out of the hole at one end or another....

① reverse sweep

② foreward sweep

③ Back bracing will push you backward and up....

④ Surfing back and forth across a hole can give you enough momentum to punch out at the end...

⑤ ...or you can punch into the trough with bow or stern...

⑥ ...and ender out!

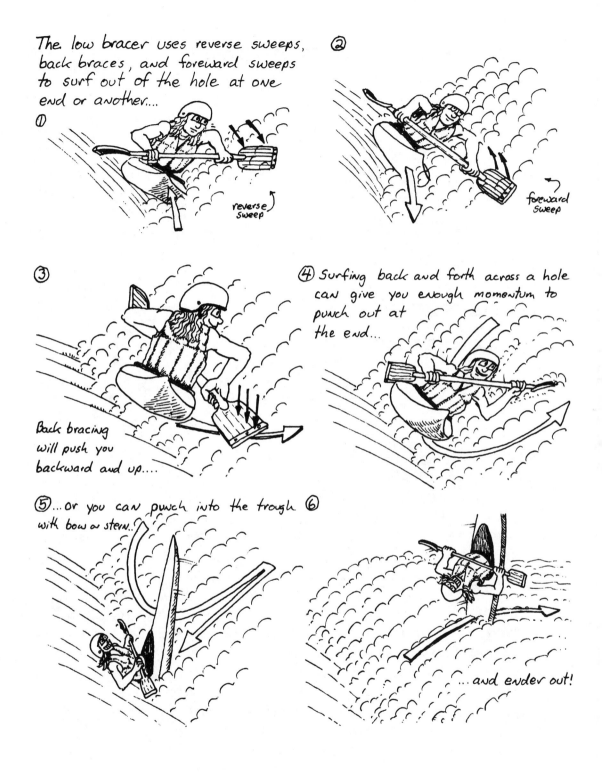

How to reduce dislocations:

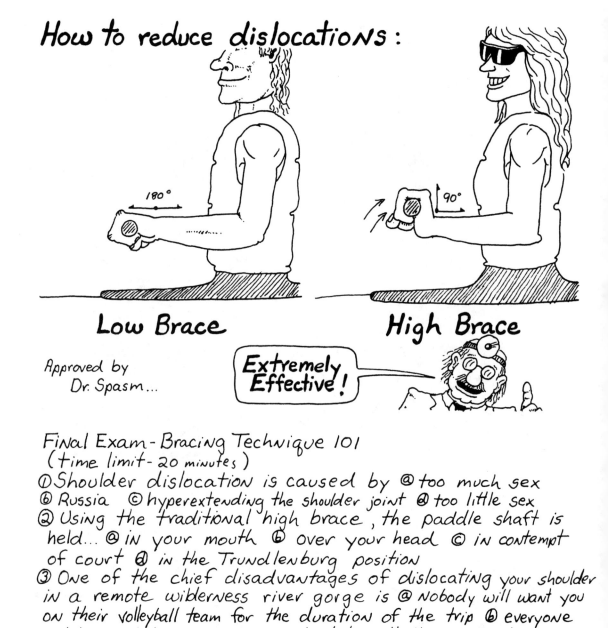

Low Brace   **High Brace**

Approved by
Dr. Spasm...

Extremely Effective!

Final Exam - Bracing Technique 101
(time limit - 20 minutes)

① Shoulder dislocation is caused by ⓐ too much sex
ⓑ Russia ⓒ hyperextending the shoulder joint ⓓ too little sex

② Using the traditional high brace, the paddle shaft is
held... ⓐ in your mouth ⓑ over your head ⓒ in contempt
of court ⓓ in the Trundlenburg position

③ One of the chief disadvantages of dislocating your shoulder
in a remote wilderness river gorge is ⓐ Nobody will want you
on their volleyball team for the duration of the trip ⓑ everyone
will be mad because you had to take all their recreational
drugs in order to get a good nights sleep ⓒ intense pain,
shock, nerve damage, etc ⓓ all of the above

④ My kayak instructor (an <u>Expert!</u>) taught me to use the high
brace exclusively on the river. I should... ⓐ buy him a box of

candy ⓑ ignore his advice ⓒ report him to the A.W.A. White-water Medical Ethics Review Board ⓓ actually try low bracing next time I go paddling and make up my own mind.

⑤ Which bracing technique offers the least danger of shoulder trauma, is more efficient, and makes hole playing more enjoyable? ⓐ high bracing ⓑ low bracing ⓒ stock car racing ⓓ computer interfacing ⓔ tennis shoe lacing

⑥ This phoney exam is yet another shameless attempt by the author to brainwash the paddling community in general and the kayaking community in particular! ⓐ True ⓑ False

⑦ If someone in my party dislocates his/her shoulder we should immediately treat for shock and ⓐ give victim plenty of whiskey and soporifics ⓑ tie rocks to the affected arm and dangle it off a ledge to pop the joint back in place ⓒ read a good first aid book and learn dislocation reduction protocol and reduce the dislocation ⓓ check and see if an ex-football coach is in our party because coaches always know what to do ⓔ immobilize the affected limb and seek expert medical treatment

⑧ Shoulder dislocation can be avoided by not ⓐ drinking too much beer and wrecking the van ⓑ high bracing in holes ⓒ eating too many poisonous mushrooms ⓓ thinking clean thoughts ⓔ putting the make on cute raft guides

⑨ When low bracing the paddle shaft is never held higher than ⓐ the epidermis ⓑ a kite ⓒ your chin ⓓ 8,000 meters

⑩ If you actually tried the High Brace Simulator Experiment add ten points for each broken tooth.

Finish

Answers: ① c, ② b, ③ c, ④ d, ⑤ b, ⑥ True, ⑦ e, ⑧ Board e, ⑨ c, ⑩ Stupid! Each correct answer counts 10 points.

Riverese

Riverese cont'd.

Appalachia – A river-rich mountainous region stretching from N. Alabama to Maine. Appalachia is where most of the S.E.'s best whitewater is. Inhabited by a somewhat sociopathic tribe of white people (mainly). Non-Southern boaters may find visiting Appalachia to be not unlike visiting precolonial New Guinea.

Awesome – impressive and inspirational. Along with "ultimate", one of the most overused of whitewater adjectives. 80's equivalent → "Atomic"

backender – A backwards ender where the boat stands vertically on its stern end. See "ender"

bad – means "good", although sometimes bad is bad, as in "a bad swim".

bankfull – Refers to water level, bankfull means high water but the river is still within its normal banks. The next stage up is floodstage.

bank scout – to scout a rapid from the bank. See "boat scout"

big water – Extremely high volume whitewater. A.K.A. "Western style water." The New River Gorge (3'+) is the S.E.'s best known big water river.

boat scout – to visually inspect a rapid by eddy-hopping it in stages and looking at obstacles as you go along. This is a fairly safe method of scouting on low to medium gradient streams but totally unsafe on high gradient streams and/or blind drops. A boater who runs a blind drop without bank scouting is known as a "rapid probe unit".

boulder – An exceptionally large rock (usually VW bug size and up)

boulder garden – A rapid or shoal that is heavily obstructed by boulders.

canoe – A.K.A. "open boat", "pig boat" – an elongated symmetrical open river craft with a rigid hull. A canoe with a deck is referred to as a "decked canoe". See "C-boat" canoeist - A.K.A. "open boater." Anyone who paddles an open canoe. Tandem canoeists are known for their constant, loud repartee concerning whose fault it was that the boat got flipped. Solo canoeists are well-known for their smug attitudes regarding all decked boaters, particularly kayakers. Recognized by their total lack of fear when swimming in Class V water. Usually heard saying "Shit, that's easy with two blades." Thought of as being obnoxious and demented by most kayakers, open boaters are useful in river rescues when not being rescued themselves. Even though canoes can run anything a decked boat can (despite what they think out West) open boaters are very insecure about the capabilities of their chosen river craft. It is the sacred duty of all kayakers to tease canoeists.

C-boat - A decked canoe. A C-1 is a single person boat and is usually paddled by mature-but-macho individuals. A C-2 is paddled by two persons who constantly scream at each other. A C-2 paddled by a married couple is usually referred to as a "D-I-V-O-R-C-E Boat."

C-boater - Possibly the most butch of all whitewater personality types, C-boaters think all other boaters are wimps, period. Kayakers are considered to be beneath contempt. When not crawling around on hands and knees at the takeout sobbing "my ankles... my knees..." they can be observed icepicking unattended kayaks in the parking area. Non C-boaters consider C-boaters to be a misguided and masochistic lot.

C.F.S. - "cubic feet per second", A.K.A. "cubes". The total volume of water passing an established point of reference on a creek or river.

chicken route - A.K.A. "sneak" - the easiest or safest route through a rapid. See "hero route"

crash and burn - Any especially picturesque wipeout in a rapid. A good crash and burn results in the boater, boat, paddle and miscellaneous equipment being scattered all over the pool below. A.K.A. "The Class VI Experience".

creek - a diminutive river. A "creek" in the S.E. usually refers to

Riverese, cont'd.

a low volume - high gradient semi-hair run. See "creek boater"

creek boater - A special breed of whitewater boater who prefers paddling steep little-known mountain creeks with a friend to slamdancing on overcrowded rivers. Although frequently criticized as being secretive, obnoxious control-freaks, creek boaters are in reality the Renaissance men (and women) of whitewater paddling. The typical creek boater is sensitive, tasteful, intelligent, urbane, discreet, and totally fearless. The creek boater prefers his women hot, his beer cold and his steak rare. In that order.

cruising river - A big river that is usually runnable year-round and doesn't require an expedition to run. A few of the Southeast's classic cruising rivers are; French Broad, Haw, James, and Potomac.

decked canoe - see "C-boat", "C-boater"

deck dancing - A relatively new addition to the universe of river stunts. Deck dancing involves clustering boats in a big hole and performing various feats of skill on the decks of the stuck boats. Handstands, headstands and raft-mooning are but a few of the tricks in the serious deck dancer's repertoire....

deck dancing

dorkus maximus - A.K.A. "turkey", "wimp", "nebbish", "geek", "neednoid", "bozo", "pinhead", "pencil neck", "maggot", "wuss", "scumbag", "dork", "nark" etc.
Derogatory term used to describe particularly nerdish paddlers. Recognized for saying stuff like "Don't you think two cases of beer is enough for <u>tonight</u>?", "I hope the ranger doesn't walk up and bust you guys", "lighting a fire with gasoline is just plain stupid!" and the classic dorkian phrase, "A chainsaw isn't a TOY!!"

drop - Any vertical change in the riverbed. A vertical drop higher than six feet is usually referred to as a waterfall.

dynamic - used to describe an extreme form of anything. Ex.-
"dynamic surfing", "dynamic peelout", etc.

eat it - To fall over in a rapid and/or to take a nasty swim. Variations include; chewed, crash and burned, creamed, body-surfed,
crunched, douched, devoured, mauled, munched, slam dunked, stuffed,
trashed, woofed, etc.

eddy - The relatively calm spots found on the downstream sides of
rocks, pilings, etc. Eddies are to boaters what trenches are to soldiers,
sanctuary for resting or scouting. On flooded or big water rivers
eddies can become whirlpool-like boat traps. See "eddy fence"

eddy-hop - to descend a rapid in
stages by catching eddies sequen-
tially.

eddy at normal water

Eddy fence - A.k.a "eddy wall", "interface". A high water phenomenon, the eddy becomes superelevated or super depressed in relation to the main current. A
seething hydraulic-like wall (interface) separates the eddy current from the
main current. The eddy itself may have
become a veritable whirlpool, double-
trapping a boater that manages to
cross the interface without getting trashed.
Once in the eddy the boater must escape
the whirlpool and the interface to get
back into the main current.

ender - A.k.a. "getting air", "Endo" (western) This is standing the boat
on end in holes or on waves. Some call an ender a "pop-up" if you
don't get shot all the way out of the water or if you fail to get perfectly
perpendicular. I never can figure out where a pop-up ends and an
ender begins, so I refer to both as enders. A good ender is where
you get tossed all the way out of the water and land upside-down.
A great ender is where you land upright on your buddies' boats back
in the holding pattern. An ender with a half-twist is a pirouette.

155

Riverese, cont'd.

How you lean when endering pretty much determines how you'll land.
Leaning foreward usually results in an upside-down landing (fig a). Leaning backward may keep the boat upright on landing (fig b). The same is pretty much true with backendering except the lean directions are reversed. Leaning back over the stern flips you back upstream (upsidedown), fig c. Leaning foreward shifts the long-axis center of gravity of the boat towards the bow and will probably result in an upright landing (fig d).
To pirouette, crossdraw as soon as you're perpendicular (fig e).

fig a   fig. b

fig c

fig. e

entrapment - A.K.A. "pinning" - Entrapment is getting stuck on an obstacle in moving water (in or out of your boat).

foot entrapment

broach

vertical pin

Any type of pinning should be considered to be a life or death emergency situation. Rescue must be quick and decisive. Often in the case of broaching or vertical pinning, the victim has a few seconds to exit his/her boat before the hull collapses or the boat planes into the flow. Scouting is the best way to avoid an entrapment situation. Many entrapments occur as the result of a paddler "just going for it" and getting stuck on an obstacle that scouting would have revealed. Articles on entrapment rescue techniques can be found in the A.W.A. Journal and in the River Safety Task Force Newsletter. Read them.

Eskimo Roll - A self rescue technique used by competent decked and open boaters to re-right the boat after a flip. Rolling is accomplished by executing a series of underwater paddle strokes while performing some intricate body english. Having a reliable roll on the river will save you (and your friends) lots of time and unnecessary risk when boating.

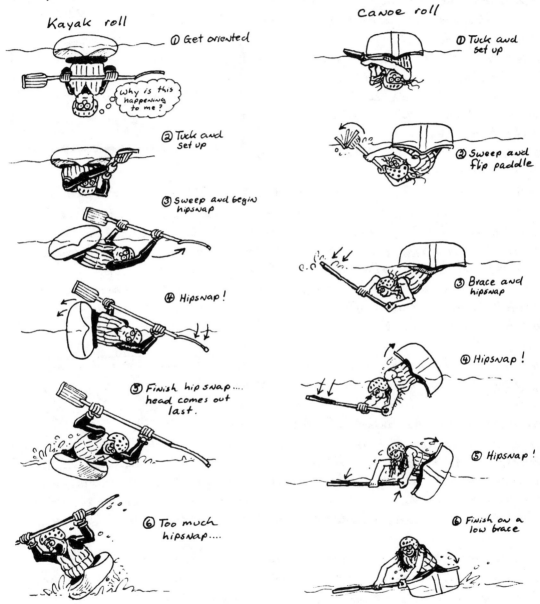

Kayak roll

① Get oriented

"Why is this happening to me?"

② Tuck and set up

③ Sweep and begin hipsnap

④ Hipsnap!

⑤ Finish hip snap.... head comes out last.

⑥ Too much hipsnap....

Canoe roll

① Tuck and set up

② Sweep and flip paddle

③ Brace and hipsnap

④ Hipsnap!

⑤ Hipsnap!

⑥ Finish on a low brace

Riverese, cont'd.

Expert boater - A self-conferred title, the qualifications for "expert" status are nebulous and vary regionally. An expert boater can be: Any boater with a reliable river roll, anyone who paddles the Gauley and lives, anyone who owns or works in a whitewater specialty shop, any raft guide, any outfitter, or anyone who writes river guidebooks. Boaters who wear "canoe instructor" patches on their lifejackets are automatically excluded from the holy realm of expert boater status (see "Dorkus Maximus"). There is no such thing as an expert flatwater boater.

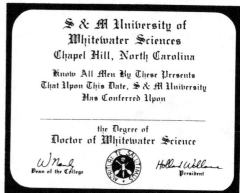

S & M University of
Whitewater Sciences
Chapel Hill, North Carolina

Know All Men By These Presents
That Upon This Date, S & M University
Has Conferred Upon

_____

the Degree of
Doctor of Whitewater Science

W Neal   Holland Williams
Dean of the College   President

↑ clip and save

Falls (water fall)- any vertical drop higher than six feet. Running waterfalls is a science, requiring a steady nerve, a calculating eye and a certain "It's a good day to die" mind-set. This is radical empiricism at its best: when running a big waterfall the boater is simultaneously both the scientist and the white rat. Although waterfall-related fatalities are rare, injuries are not. Waterfalls up to 45 feet have been successfully run in the Southeast by members of the whitewater community's lunatic fringe.

flatwater - Any water that is still or flows in a slovenly and sluggish manner. Normal whitewater boaters look forward to paddling flatwater with the same enthusiasm they have for contracting herpes. Surprisingly, in some parts of the country flatwater paddling is done for "fun" and is even considered a "sport" by some! Flatwater paddlers eat alfalfa sprouts by choice, prefer gatorade to beer, and think a low brace is an ace bandage worn below the knee. See "dorkus maximus."

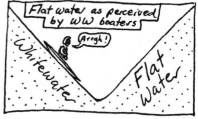

Flat water as perceived by WW boaters

Arrgh!

Whitewater

Flat Water

funny water - Mostly found on floodstage or "big water" rivers, funny water is usually anything but! Found where pools or eddies normally would be, funny water manifests itself as whirlpools, mobile eddy

158

walls, percolating eddies and exploding waves. Funny water is generally experienced in this way..... you're running a river at high water. You clean the hardest rapid on the river, hit the pool at the bottom and relax. Suddenly something grabs your boat, flips you, and tears you out of your boat. You go for a nasty swim in the "pool."

whew...

funny water

Gradient - Refers to the steepness of the riverbed. Expressed as the average drop in feet per mile. Low gradient rivers drop less than 20 feet per mile (New R. Gorge), medium gradient rivers drop 35 to 50 feet per mile (Ocoee, Gauley). True high gradient creeks and rivers drop in excess of 100 feet per mile (Wilson Creek, Wautauga River, Overflow Creek, etc.

Hair - dangerous and difficult whitewater. A hair river possesses a combination of high gradient, high volume and extreme technical difficulty. Deadly obstacles abound and rescue is difficult or impossible. Some classic hair runs in the Southeast are: Chattooga IV above 4.0', Upper Nantahala (high), Wilson Creek above 1', Lower Meadow River (optimal), Russel Fork (ky.) (high), Upper Yok (high), Wautauga (high), Overflow Creek (optimal).

HBO-Bio - As in "Last weekend we ran the HBO-Bio". Translation: "Last weekend we watched whitewater slides and movies and drank beer." Watching enough slide shows and movies eventually allows the boater to engage in "merc-talk" about rivers the boater has never run. Example: "Lava is just a big water Class III! What's the big deal?"

helmet - "brain bucket" - Rigid head protection device worn by paddlers to prevent non-drug related brain damage.

hero route - the hardest imaginable route through a given rapid.

hole - see "hydraulic"

Riverese, cont'd.

hole extraction - pulling a paddler out of a hole he or she is stuck in.

hole hog - A boater who stays in a play hole too long, forcing others to wait an excessive amount of time to play in said hole. The accepted rule of thumb for length of stay in a hole is two minutes minus 5 seconds for each boater in the holding pattern (Ocoee Rules).

holding pattern - the elliptical line of boaters playing in or waiting to play in a play hole or play wave. An overcrowded holding pattern in an eddy is referred to as a "fully-stacked" holding pattern or eddy.

hurricane season - Late August thru October hurricanes and big tropical depressions make landfall and track inland to pump up rivers and creeks which at this time of year are exceptionally low from lack of rain.

hydraulic - A.K.A. "hole", "sousehole", "vertical eddy", "reversal" etc. Hydraulics are caused by water passing over an obstacle and creating a recirculating upstream flow below. Hydraulics come in an infinite variety and are a source of amusement and/or fear for boaters. A hole used as an eddy is referred to as a "keeper eddy". Breaking waves are often mistaken for holes but they lack a recirculating flow downstream of the wave face. See "wave".

kayak - A.k.a. "yak", "k-1" kayaks are the most common kind of river craft and are probably the easiest boat to master. Kayaks are distinguishable from C-1's in that C-boaters kneel and use a single-bladed paddle while kayakers sit and use a two-bladed paddle.

C-1

Kayak

kayaker - "yak jockey", "river maggot" In the words of an open-boater friend of mine..... "twice the paddle, half the man", kayakers are perceived by non-kayakers as; ① the watery equivalent of

Hell's Angels, or ② brain-damaged river loonies, or both. Easily recognized on the river for their penchant for traveling in large, loud groups and surfing every wave or hole on the river no matter how small. Kayakers have a reputation for peeling out in front of canoes and rafts, getting run over by canoes, rafts and other kayakers while surfing holes, and/or mooning rafters and open boaters. Kayakers view all other types of river craft as slow-moving impediments to wave and hole playing. Canoeists are occasionally tolerated by kayakers for their entertainment value when they perform canoe crash and burns in every other rapid. Decked canoeists (particularly C-1 paddlers) are tolerated by kayakers primarily for their verbal abuse value if they eat it in front of the kayakers.

keeper eddy - See "hydraulic", "eddy fence"

local(s) Recognized by "Goin' fishin'?" or "If you leave your car here I'm gonna blow it up!" Locals are the people indigenous to whatever area you happen to be in. Generally friendly when treated with respect. Locals in Appalachia tend to look upon whitewater boating as an activity ranking somewhere between devil worship and heroin addiction. See "Appalachia"

lunch bunny - A.K.A. "lunch fairy", "female guide trainee". Not to be confused with the true woman raft guide, lunch bunnies are there to provide a little T&A for the customers and to show that even on the river, a woman's place is in the kitchen. Disgusting.

mega- prefix used to describe anything big and/or powerful... mega-hole, mega-boulder, mega-dork, etc.

mercenary - Any river guide, outfitter, or paddler gainfully employed (or gainfully unemployed) in the River Industry. When not paddling or sleeping, mercenaries engage in "merc-talk", an esoteric verbal ritual.

merc-talk - Ritualized form of communication between experts, raft guides and outfitters. This involves relating river stories in anecdotal

Riverese, cont'd.

form. Sample; Merc #1: "I was running some carp down Big Sandy at 5' and I flipped the boat in a hole 'cause the customers were air-bracing". Merc #2: "Wow.. 5 feet! That's high for civilians!" Merc #3: "I flipped a raft full of stewardesses on the Cheat last April when it was running 7 feet. Thing was, one of 'em got hypothermic and I had to spend an hour in a bivy bag with her and..." Merc #2 "I was running The Canyon last spring at 65,000 cfs with a group of registered nurses and...." Merc #1 "I heard Crystal got changed last year. Did it?" etc

mobile strainer - A tree, railroad tie, telephone pole, etc. floating down a floodstage river with you.

open boater - see "canoeist"

patazod - Contraction of "Patagonia" and "Izod". Refers to any type of designer outdoor clothing and/or people who wear two or more art-icles of said clothing. A.K.A. "River Preppie"

↳ sew on paddling jacket

peelout - Exiting an eddy pointed upstream. When you cross the eddyline the current snatches your bow and you do a dynamic 180° turn if you remember to brace and lean on your downstream side. Otherwise you'll flip dynamically. See "eat it"

pillow - A reactionary cushion of water on the upstream face of rocks and boulders. Can be surfed on a downstream brace in tight situations. Riding a poorly-cushioned or highly aeriated pillow can result in a broach.

pin - see "Entrapment"

pirouette - See "Ender"

typical pillow

pool - Calm water above or below a rapid or drop

pourover - A.K.A. "washover" A semi-submerged rock or ledge with a small amount of water passing over it and (usually) a nasty hydraulic just below. Hard to recognize from upstream until you start over the top ("event horizon") and realize you're fixing to get trashed! Often preceeded by an "F.L.W." (see "waves") pourovers look like big rounded waves from upstream.

oh shit!

typical pourover

"Event Horizon"

put in - The place where you get out of the car and get into your boat.

raft - A.K.A. "rubber bus", "cattle boat", etc. A large, cumbersome, semi-rigid inflatable platform used primarily for transporting civilians down rivers on a commercial basis. While having a reputation for running over kayakers and generally cluttering up the river, rafts can carry vast quantities of food and beer when used in kayak support mode.

raft guide - aka. "captain", "boatman" etc. The man or woman responsible for yelling at the customers in rapids and entertaining them the rest of the time. Needless to say, most raft guides are semi-psychotic most of the time. When not rigging rafts, packing or unpacking lunch, guiding, or sleeping, raft guides engage in "merc-talk", plot guide strikes, and plan trips to The Grand, Costa Rica or Nepal.

rafters - "Carp" (upper Yok), "civilians", "customers", "pilgrims", "touroids", "raftoids", "creeps from Ohio", etc. Rafters are people who pay money to get yelled at by raft guides. When not engaged in water fights, yelling contests, and speculations on when lunch will be served, rafters can be seen running rapids with their paddles in the air. Often resented by private boaters, rafters provide a good livelihood for river people and give us all somebody to look down on.

rapid - A.K.a. "rapids" - A section of the river characterized by increased gradient, fast water, waves, holes, and assorted other obstacles.

rebar - metal reinforcement rods used in construction of dams, bridges, etc. When a concrete structure breaks down it leaves rebar-studded

Riverese, contd

death traps in the river.

river left - a.k.a. "left" On the left facing downstream. See "river right"

river right - a.k.a. "right" On the right facing downstream. See "river left"

river maggot - Derogatory term describing decked boats (kayakers in particular) infesting play spots on rivers.

roostertail - A fountain-like liquid obstacle caused by fast-moving water striking an obstacle and spewing in an upwardly direction.

safety rope - a.k.a. "throw rope", "rescue rope", "rapid floss" - The essential piece of river safety equipment! Safety ropes should be carried in each boat when running rivers of Class III or greater difficulty. Throw bags have become the most popular type of safety rope and like the traditional coiled throw rope, throw bags require practice to use properly and safely.

Throw Bag

Throw Rope

scouting - to visually inspect a rapid. Bank scouting is done on foot. Boat scouting is done from the boat while eddy-hopping the rapid in short segments.

shoal - Any shallow ledgy rapid

shuttle - a.k.a. "hide and seek" This is the pre-run arranging of motor vehicles, people, and boats in such a way as to leave a vehicle or vehicles at the takeout to enable you to retrieve the vehicle or vehicles you left at the putin after the run.

Shuttle protocol - Since boaters often find themselves waiting impatiently

at a rendezvous point for other boaters to arrive (in six different cars) to run shuttle, here are a few guidelines for waiting time for other boaters once a quorum has been reached ("Quorum" is defined as the minimum number of motorized vehicles needed to run the shuttle, i.e - two) and the other guys are unnecessary: "...10 minutes more..." - casual acquaintances, women boaters, anyone traveling less than fifty miles to the river, wife or husband
"....20 more minutes." - full professors, doctors, pretty good friends, women boaters, anyone traveling more than 100 miles to run the river.
"...30 more minutes" - very good friends, team pharmacologist, very attractive women boaters, anyone traveling more than 200 miles to run the river
"...one hour and not a minute more!" best boating buddies, girlfriends, boyfriends, famous boaters, magazine writers, politicians, media personalities, team pharmacologist, the expert boater who runs this river all the time that you want to follow down in the hairy stuff, anyone traveling more than 250 miles to run the river.

shuttle bunny - Someone's wife or girlfriend who runs the shuttle and waits patiently while you run the river. "Gee Hon', this isn't the Nantahala...I think it would be safer if you didn't run today - this is a ~~tough~~ run!" Poof! instant shuttlebunny. Male equivalent - "shuttle monkey"

Sieve - As in "boulder sieve"- A strainer created by a jumble of boulders.

Ski-jump - To use the lip of a drop as a launching pad. The idea here is to paddle hard to gain momentum and shoot over whatever lies below; keeper hydraulic, pointy rocks, etc.

Ski-jumping a bad hole

slam dance - What happens in fully-stacked eddies when overcrowding results in hand to hand combat with elbows and paddles.

slam dunk - A.K.a. "stuffed" - Refers to what happens when a paddler runs a steep drop and gets jammed into the very bottom of the hole below. The paddler disappears, gets trashed and is spit out piece by piece.

Sluice - Any narrow eddy-less channel in a rapid.

sneak - To take the chicken route through a rapid. Also means to covertly portage a rapid.

Speared - getting stabbed in the upper body by the bow or stern of a decked boat. Usually occurs in eddies and crowded play spots.

squirt boat - An extremely radical low-volume decked boat that can ender, back ender, and pirouette on eddylines and in flatwater.

squirtable - refers to the ability of a radical hull to perform various submarine and aerial maneuvers.

stopper - A hole or breaking wave that causes an abrupt cessation of your downstream progress.

strainer - Any obstacle on the river that allows water to pass through but not boats and people. Downed trees, logjams, and boulder sieves are the most common form of strainer. See "entrapment"

surf - to ride a wave on its upstream face or to get stuck in a hole (intentionally or unintentionally). Hole surfing is easier than wave surfing because once you're in the hole, it does all the work.

T-bone - To plow into a rock, boat or raft at a 90° angle to the obstacle. T-boning a raft can cause traumatic deflation of the raft. T-boning a rock can result in a bow ding or a broken ankle. T-boning a kayaker can result in a broken face.

takeout - Where you get out of your boat and into a car.

tongue - "vee", "slick" A smooth V-shaped strip of water indicating (usually) deep water and a clean line through a rapid.

tuber - A.K.A. "hole bait", "dead meat" A tuber is a root-like vegetable or someone who runs rivers in innertubes, usually without benefit of helmet, lifejacket, and common sense. Despite the charming egalitarian aspects of the "sport", inner tubing is proof that natural selection is still hard at work.

turkey - Somewhat outdated derogatory term. See "dorkus maximus", "rafter", "tuber"

twilight zoned - A common mental affliction of whitewater boaters. Symptoms include confusion, paranoia, and intense anxiety. Example: a boater still wearing his wetsuit walks into the Bryson City "Piggly Wiggly" to buy some beer and begins to think he's an alien from Cygnus 3 because everyone in the store freezes and stares when he walks in. Often boaters get twilight zoned when driving in Appalachia at night. Suddenly you can't remember if this is West Virginia or North Carolina. Your friends can't seem to remember which state you're in either. Fortunately there is a fairly reliable method for narrowing down your approximate location: Look at your dashboard- whatever guidebook is on top of all the other dashboard flora is probably the guidebook for the state you're in. Open it to where the biggest beer stain is and chances are that's where you are.

undercut - A rock formation or boulder that has been eroded just below the surface of the water. Extremely dangerous for paddlers, undercuts are often invisible until you find yourself being flushed under one.

vee - wave - See "wave"

vee-hole - A converging hole that caves in on you from both sides and usually dynamically flips you.

Vee-hole

Riverese, cont'd

walk the dog – To portage a rapid, drag your boat, or covertly indulge in controlled substances (A.K.A. "safety meeting")

washed out – High water phenomenon wherein most of the obstacles in a rapid are submerged and the rapid becomes technically easier.

wave – The direct expression of the river's energy. Waves come in a wide variety of shapes and sizes. Below are some of the most common wave "types":

brain wave – A percolating wave often found on big water or floodstage rivers. See "funny water"

breaking wave – a.k.a. "wave/hole" A wave that breaks all the way down its upstream face. Unlike a hole, breaking waves lack a recirculating flow downstream of the wave face.

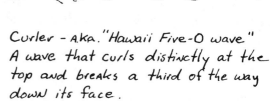

Curler – a.k.a. "Hawaii Five-O wave" A wave that curls distinctly at the top and breaks a third of the way down its face.

diagonal wave – usually seen at high water levels, diagonal waves are caused by an obstruction downstream of the wave or a sharp curve in the river. These are notorious raft-flippers. A.k.a. "lateral wave". See "reaction wave".

Aiiieeee!

explosion wave - A high water phenomenon, these waves have a cycle: The wave starts building up (fig 1), reaches maximum height and curls over (fig 2), then caves in and begins re-forming. Commonly found at the bottom of rapids on floodstage rivers among big offset waves.

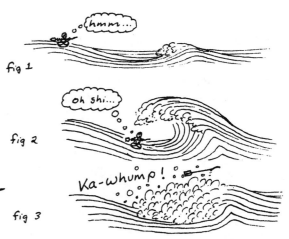

fig 1 ○○(hmm...

fig 2 oh shi...

fig 3 Ka-whump! ○○○

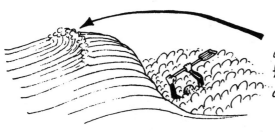

F.L.W. - aka. "funny little wave". These are small curlers found on the upstream faces of the humps immediately pre-ceeding pourovers and big holes.

Offset waves - When small, offset waves are referred to as "chop", which makes for an awkward, bumpy ride in a decked boat (Ocoee @ 2,000 cfs). When large these waves are concave and violent. The boater gets tossed from one wave to the next like a hacky-sack.

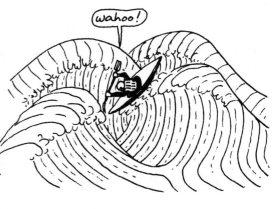

wahoo!

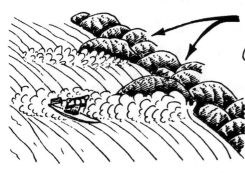

Reaction wave - Aka. "bank wave", "veflex wave", "lateral wave" Big breaking waves (usually diagonal) that are the result of the current striking an obstacle and bouncing off. Found on big water or floodstage rivers near river banks or megaboulders. Also found on the outside of a curve on the river.

Riverese cont'd.

riffles - Usually found at the top of rapids at high water, the river's velocity increases to form these big rounded waves. a.k.a. "rollers"

Standing waves - stationary waves in sets of two or more. Big standing waves are often referred to as "hay stacks". Standing waves are caused by the river giving up its energy as the current is slowed down for one reason or another.

Tailwaves - the series of standing waves at the bottom of many rapids. At high water this is where you usually find explosion waves and funny water.

Whitewater divorce - What happens when one member of a couple gets fed up with tandem open boating and buys a kayak, C-1 or solo canoe.

Window-shaded (West Coast terminology) Describes what happens when a paddler flips on his/her upstream side while side-surfing a big hole. Southeastern boaters refer to this phenomenon as "dynamic rolling" or "washing machining".

Zoo - A.k.a. "Six Flags Over Neoprene" - Term used to describe any particularly crowded river or playspot. Examples; Nantahala Falls (summer), Ocoee (summer), New River Gorge (spring, summer), Gauley (fall releases), Lower Yok (summer), etc.